IATLIS Series : 1

RESEARCH IN LIBRARY
AND
INFORMATION SCIENCE IN INDIA

RESEARCH IN LIBRARY
AND
INFORMATION SCIENCE IN INDIA

(A bibliography of Ph D, M Phil and MLIS dissertations)

Compiled by
P S G KUMAR

Indexed by
A TEJOMURTY
and
H R CHOPRA

CONCEPT PUBLISHING COMPANY, NEW DELHI

First Published 1987

Published by

Naurang Rai
Concept Publishing Company
H-13 Bali Nagar
NEW DELHI-110 015 (India)

Printed in India by

Printway India
at S. Narayan & Sons
7117/18 Pahari Dhiraj,
DELHI-110 006

FOREWORD

Dr. P S G Kumar and his colleagues have made a commendable effort in this publication to document research in library and information science done under the aegis of departments for the subject in different Indian universities.

Dr. Kumar is well suited to be the guiding spirit for such a task as he himself has earned a doctorate in the subject and heads the department in Nagpur University.

The team's efforts to collect information evidently did not meet with complete success. However, this does not detract from the value of this book which also provides us with an analysis of the data.

The Association of Indian Universities regularly brings out Bibliography of doctoral dissertations and reports new ones in the issues of the University News. The apex professional organisations in the country should now follow the cue given here.

1 January 1987

S.P. Agrawal
Director
NASSDOC-ICSSR
35, Ferozshah Road
New Delhi-110001

PREFACE

There are about 38 Universities in India providing Master of Library and Information Science Course and 18 Universities having research facilities in Library and Information Science. In many of the library and information schools, submission of a dissertation in lieu of one paper is a common feature at the MLIS level. Library and Information Science in India has come of age now, and the need for a bibliography of library science research done in India has become imperative, both from the point of view of knowing what work has been done in our universities, and also from the point of view of avoidance of duplication of effort. The present work precisely aims at satisfying this long-felt requirement.

An attempt was made to gather information from the various library schools of our country, regarding the MLIS and Ph D dissertations. Despite repeated reminders and efforts, information regarding the research guides could not be obtained in many cases. Similarly, a few library schools did not provide us complete information regarding the dissertations. So, the present bibliography cannot and does not claim to be a comprehensive one, and neither we intend to do so. It is only a beginning in this direction, and we shall feel happily rewarded if the present work puts its first step, though modest but a firm one, and be of help to the library personnel in general and the library and information science faculty, researchers, and students in particular.

All those people who have acceeded to our request and obliged us by giving the required information, despite their busy time and professional involvement, deserve acknowledgement and thanks, and we gratefully do so.

Lastly one more word with you. In the Introduction following this page we gave an analysis of the entries. It had been our endeavour to make the work as comprehensive as possible. Towards this end, we have been adding new entries from time to time. This might have resulted in little variation of the statistical data. However, it will give fairly good idea about the trend in research in library and information science in India.

NAGPUR,
1 January 1987

P S G KUMAR
A TEJOMURTY
H R CHOPRA

INTRODUCTION

Information is an essential ingredient of the socio-economic fabric of any country. If there is a distinct socio-economic structure for a country there will also be a distinct information structure governing this. The development of documentation and information services in a country is very much in consonance with her national development activities. In fact, the tempo of these services is a factor of the intensity of the country's research and development endeavour. A natural consequence of the tremendous national research efforts and activities in different disciplines of knowledge was the demand for active library, documentation and information services at different levels. The first one-year post-graduate diploma course in library science was started in the Madras University in 1937 under the leadership of S.R. Ranganathan. The University of Delhi was the first in India to start one-year master's degree in library science in 1948 (though initially it was called B Lib Sc). Its name was changed to M Lib Sc in 1949. With the growing need for library services, the need for well qualified library personnel also started increasing, the result being the proliferation of library science schools. Today library and information science is a well-recognised discipline, and the training programme is today available in about 58 Indian universities, out of which about 38 have provision for master's course.

At the time of the commencement of the M Lib Sc course in the University of Delhi in 1948 under the leadership of Ranganathan, the role of research oriented education was fully realised, and developmental research was made an integral part of the said course. The idea of the project report/literature survey/dissertation was to bring out the inherent skills of the students. While preparing the project report the student is expected to apply his knowledge he has acquired during his formal training, and work seriously on a topic, and submit a dissertation. This work is done under the guidance and supervision of a faculty member or an outside expert. In many cases, the problems chosen for dissertation were to contribute to the development of new techniques and/or solving the library problems of immediate focus. This pattern of the Delhi University M Lib Sc dissertation gradually spread to other Indian universities which started similar courses. Despite timely changes in the M Lib Inf Sc syllabi of different universities, the research project remained an integral constituent of the curriculum in almost all our library schools.

1. SCOPE

Bibliographic organization of research output is a must in any discipline. The number of dissertations submitted as part of the MLIS curriculum in Indian universities has been on a steady increase. To keep track of the growth, not much bibliographical work has been done. An attempt is made here to systematically analyse the MLIS dissertations and Ph D theses of various Indian library schools. The listing is available, in some cases, up to 1985, from the inception of M Lib Sc course in each particular library school. Though complete coverage has been aimed at, this work does not claim total comprehensiveness. In some cases information provided by the departments has been inadequate and incomplete. The listing provided in this work is based on the information made available by the various library schools. It is possible that in some cases the figures need updating.

2. ARRANGEMENT

The whole work is arranged under four sections, spread over nine parts. Section A consists of MLIS dissertations. The alphabetical subject part of Section A arranges entries alphabetically by title, giving detailed information about the author, name of the institution, year, and the name of the supervisor. Name index (part 2), and institutionwise index (part 3) of MLIS dissertations refer to the alphabetical subject part of Section A. Section B covers doctoral theses. The doctoral degrees awarded to library science personnel under different disciplines are listed in part 4. Name index (part 5), institutionwise index (part 6) and guidewise index (part 7) to doctoral theses provide linkage references to part 4 of Section B. Section C comprises of only one part (part 8), and lists 13 M Phil dissertations. Section D deals with Doctoral Research in Progress consisting of 52 items. After having completed the bibliographical work, we have received some information from different library schools very late. Hence, this information is added in the form of appendix. Appendix one provides information about MLIS dissertations of Andhra University, Nagpur University (1984-1985), Osmania University, Punjab University (1984-1985), University of Poona, and Vikram University (1984-1985). Under each university, MLIS dissertations are arranged yearwise, sub-arrangement being alphabetical by author. The number of entries in Appendix one is 210. These are in addition to 1431 entries in Section A, Part I, thus taking the total of MLIS dissertations to 1641. Appendix two has information about two latest (available) doctoral awards. This figure takes the total number of doctoral awards to 74 (72 entries in Section B, Part 4 plus 2 entries in Appendix 2). In all, this bibliography consists of 1780 entries, comprising of 74 entries of doctoral theses, 52 entries of doctoral research in progress, 13 M Phil dissertations, and 1641 MLIS dissertations.

3. MLIS DISSERTATIONS

3.1. Subjectwise Breakup

Though the general understanding is that an MLIS dissertation should have a library topic as its theme, in practice it is observed that a great number of research projects/dissertations/literature surveys relate to topics outside library science. The Table one reveals this.

Table one makes it clear that out of the total 1,641 MLIS dissertations, 1,025 are on library and information science, and the rest relate to other disciplines. The total number of dissertations 1,641 taken as equal to 100 library and information science dissertations numbering 1,025 contribute about 62.5 per cent, and all the other subjects make up the remaining portion, i.e., 616 dissertations having 37.5 per cent. After library and information science, generalia bibliography dominates the work area with an absolute number of 83 dissertations (5 per cent), to be followed by book science 62 (4.2 per cent). If these two subject

TABLE 1 : **Subjectwise break-up of MLIS Dissertations**

Subject	Number	Percentage
Archaeology	1	0.1
Agriculture	20	1.2
Animal husbandry	8	0.5
Anthropology	1	0.1
Biology	6	0.4
Book science	69	4.2
Botany	11	0.6
Chemistry	13	0.8
Communication	1	0.1
Economics	48	2.9
Education	48	2.9
Engineering	24	1.5
Fine Arts	11	0.6
Generalia	13	0.8
Generalia Bibliography	83	5.0
Geography	8	0.5
Geology	3	0.2
History	8	0.5
Journalism	1	0.1
Law	6	0.4
Library and Information Science	1025	62.5
Literature	12	0.7
Management Science	4	0.2
Mathematics	4	0.2
Medicine	28	1.7
Philosophy	5	0.3
Physics	14	0.8
Political Science	35	2.1
Psychology	11	0.6
Religion	6	0.4
Research methodology	3	0.2
Sciences (in general)	8	0.5
Social sciences (in general)	12	0.7
Sociology	46	2.8
Spiritual experience	1	0.1
Statistics	1	0.1
Technology	12	0.7
Universe of Knowledge	1	0.1
Useful arts	24	1.5
Zoology	6	0.4
Total	1,641	100.0

areas can be taken as allied subjects of library and information science, then the other subjects which dominate are education 48 (2.9 per cent) ; economics 48 (2.9 per cent) ; sociology 46 (2.8 per cent) ; and political science 35 (2.1 per cent). Natural science subjects do not seem to have much attraction for M Lib Inf Sc dissertations.

3.2. Library and Information Science Dissertations

Table two makes it clear that there are 1,025 dissertations which have library and information science as their theme. It should be interesting to know which facets of library and infor-

TABLE 2 : **Break-up of Library and Information Science Dissertations**

Area of study	Number	Percentage
Academic libraries :		
— college libraries	97	9.5
— research libraries	27	2.6
— school libraries	25	2.4
— university libraries	134	13.1
Associations	20	1.9
Automation	10	0.9
Business libraries	30	2.9
Cataloguing	44	4.3
Citation analysis	30	2.9
Classification	68	6.6
Conference	1	0.1
Contact libraries	1	0.1
Cooperation	14	1.4
Documentation	51	5.0
Education (Library)	26	2.6
Information	142	13.9
Library profession	20	1.9
Library science	34	3.4
Library services	26	2.5
Management	32	3.1
Public libraries	70	6.8
Reference service	28	2.7
Special libraries	35	3.5
Users survey	60	5.9
Total	1,025	100.0

mation science are more popular as far as project reports are concerned. The break up is presented in Table two.

Within the discipline of library and information science, the area 'information' seems to find maximum favour with the MLIS students for their dissertations. Here 'information' is taken to be a broad spectrum including within it studies relating to dissemination of information, information retrieval, information requirements, information sources, information services, information systems, and information technology. This area counts for 13.9 per cent with 142 out of a total of 1,025 dissertations. This may be due to the rising importance of information and its various dimensions in the present day society. Close on heels to this are studies relating to university libraries, which have 13.1 per cent with 134 dissertations. Many of the master's students, faculty members, and librarians themselves are naturally interested in university libraries, their problems and prospects, and their services. Studies relating to other areas worth mentioning are college libraries with 97 dissertations (9.5 per cent) ; and public libraries with 70 dissertations (6.8 per cent). As far as the library techniques are concerned, classification has the maximum attraction, i.e., 68 dissertations (6.6 per cent) ; users survey with 60 dissertations (5.9 per cent) ; and documentation with 51 dissertations (5 per cent).

4. DOCTORAL THESES

Provision for Ph D in library science in India was made for the first time in 1948 in the University of Delhi, under the dynamic leadership of Ranganathan. Today, about 12 Indian universities have provision for research leading to Ph D in library and information science. The first Ph D in library science was awarded (Delhi University) to Mr. D.B. Krishnarao for his work on "Facet analysis and depth classification of agriculture". His research supervisor was S.R. Ranganathan. A long period of lull followed after this. Till very recently, doctoral study in library and information science in India invited a pandora's box of silly and vexing questions about the need for and utility of such a degree. It must be clearly understood that the Ph D is a research degree, which is awarded for proof that the research scholar is qualified to pursue reflective and analytical inquiry. Of late, there has been a sudden increase in interest and enthusiasm to prosecute doctoral studies in library and information science in our country. The Indian library schools have so far awarded Ph D degree to about 41 scholars for their theses. In both the active library profession and library and information science faculty put together, there are about 74 persons who hold Ph D degree. Out of this, about 44 are Ph D degree holders in library science. Three of these are awarded degrees from foreign universities. The remaining 30 Ph D degrees are awarded for work done in departments like economics, education, history, law, political science and so on, on matters relating to library science.

4.1. Doctoral Theses in Library and Information Science

The areawise analysis of library and information science Ph Ds is presented in Table three.

TABLE 3 : **Areawise Break-up of Library Science Doctoral Theses**

Area	Number	Percentage
Academic libraries	1	2.3
Archives	1	2.3
Automation	1	2.3
Bibliometry	1	2.3
Buildings	1	2.3
Citation analysis	2	4.6
Classification	8	18.0
Cooperation	1	2.3
Documentation	1	2.3
Indexing	4	9.0
Information	3	6.7
Legislation	1	2.3
Librarianship	2	4.6
Literature survey	1	2.3
Manuscripts	1	2.3
Periodical literature	1	2.3
Public libraries	4	9.0
Reference tools	1	2.3
Resource sharing	1	2.3
Scientific and technical libraries	1	2.3
University libraries	7	15.9
Total	44	100.0

It is interesting to note that out of the total 44 Ph Ds in library and information science, classification seems to be the most dominating area, accounting for 8 theses with a percentage of 18. University libraries constitute the theme for 7 theses accounting for 15.9 per cent. Indexing with 4 theses (9 per cent); and public libraries with 4 theses (9 per cent) come next in the scale.

4.2. Chronology of Library and Information Science Doctoral Theses

The chronological growth of doctorates in library and information science in India is traced here. Commencing with the first doctorate in 1957, we have now about 41 theses (Indian schools) upto 1985. The twentynine years of research activity have produced fortyone doctorates in our discipline. Could it be considered a good rate ? The yearwise break-up is made available in Table four.

TABLE 4 : **Yearwise Break-up of Doctoral Theses**

Year	Number
1957	1
1977	1
1978	1
1979	1
1980	2
1981	1
1982	2
1983	7
1984	12
1985	13
Total	41

Table four reveals that during 1958 to 1976 there was no doctoral theses in our discipline for which the degree was awarded. From 1977 onwards we can see a continuous (though at a slow pace) submission of doctoral theses. This almost constant trend is visible upto 1982. We witness a sudden rise in the number of doctoral theses in 1983 with a figure of seven. The year 1984 accounts for 12 doctoral awards. Of course, the peak is 1985 in which year the number of awards went upto thirteen. Could it be because of the fact that the new entrants to the profession (mostly faculty) are young, dynamic, well qualified and research-minded ? Another valid reason could be the increasing value attached to a doctorate in our discipline, just like in other disciplines.

The discipline of library and information science has its own peculiarities and problems. It embraces all kinds of activities involved in the whole process of collection, organization, analysis and dissemination of information, and thereby includes a variety of problems, professionals, organizations and intellectual commitments. Hence, a summary treatment of the research work done in this field is pregnant with difficulties.

Bibliographic organization of research work is not properly and adequately being undertaken in our country. No systematic effort has been made to disseminate information on theses and dissertations submitted to the universities and institutions. However, this information is being communicated informally among the professional colleagues during conferences, seminars, etc. An enquiry into the dissertations and theses in our subject area makes it clear that a number of studies are interdisciplinary. Library and information science (or for that matter librarianship) is an integrative system. This naturally makes interdisciplinary studies imperative. This does not mean that research in librarianship cannot stand alone, or that it is not self-sufficient. Interdisciplinarity is important to research in all academic disciplines.

SECTION A

MLIS DISSERTATIONS

PART—I

ALPHABETICAL SUBJECT PART

(*MLIS DISSERTATIONS*)

Entry No.

AGRICULTURE

Bibliography

Agriculture literature published in India, 1960-70 : A select bibliography—Balbir Singh. (Punjab University, 1975). 1

Credit

Agricultural credit : Its structure and flow—K.V. Rajarao. (Andhra University, 1981). (Guide : K. Siva Reddy). 2

Crop Breeding

Breeding major crops in India—N.R. Satyanarayana. (BHU, 1971). 3

Extension

Agricultural extension in India, 1960-70 : A literature survey and trend report—P.S.G. Kumar. (BHU, 1971). (Guide : P.N. Kaula). 4

Fertilizers

Fertilizers : Their production and use—K.S. Sharma. (Andhra University, 1981). (Guide : P. Somaraju). 5

Food

Food problems in India, 1960-70 :

Entry No.

From shortage to self-sufficiency—D. Chandran.
(BHU, 1972).

Periodicals

Characteristics of Indian periodicals in agriculture—
N. Singh.
(BHU, 1979). 7

Plants

Cultivation of fruit plants in horticulture—
R.J. Upadhyay.
(BHU, 1968). 8

Glossary of minor food plants of India—H.C. Jain.
(INSDOC, 1973).
(Guide : K. Kashyap). 9

Viruses and virus diseases of plants in India :
Bibliographical study—Nirupama Gupta.
(INSDOC, 1966).
(Guide : S. Surender Mohan). 10

Oils and Oilseeds

Technological developments in the field of oils and
oilseeds in 1960-64 : A trend report—
P. Purnananda Sastry.
(INSDOC, 1966).
(Guide : S. Dutta). 11

Soil Fertility

Soil fertility—T.K. Manmohan Das.
(BHU, 1974). 12

Wheat and Rice Breeding

Breeding, cytology and genetics of wheat and rice :
A review of work done during 1960-64—
C.M. Chadha.
(INSDOC, 1966).
(Guide : B. Kamalarao). 13

Entry No.

ANIMAL HUSBANDARY

Dairy

Dairy development—M. Anuradha.
(Andhra University, 1981).
(Guide : K. Sarada). 14

Dairy science—M.S. Srivastava.
(BHU, 1968). 15

Evaluation of Dairy Science Abstracts with special reference to Indian contribution—M.M. Mishra.
(BHU, 1978). 16

Fish

Effects of pollutants of fish—D. Vijayasaradhi.
(Andhra University, 1980).
(Guide : K. Siva Reddy). 17

Fisheries in India—R.N. Singh.
(BHU). 18

Trend report on induced breeding of fishes in India—O.N. Chadha.
(INSDOC, 1968).
(Guide : S. Nagarajan). 19

Pisciculture

Recent trend in pisciculture—V. Chandrasekhararao.
(Andhra University, 1980).
(Guide : G.V.S.L.N. Raju). 20

Sheep and Wool

Research work done on sheep and wool science in India—Veera Gogia.
(Vikram University, 1973).
(Guide : S.S. Agrawal). 21

ANTHROPOLOGY

Information needs of anthropologists : A case study of Anthropological Survey of India, Mysore—Somashekhar Karnavar.

Entry No.

(University of Mysore, 1980).
(Guide : N.B. Pangannaya). 22

BIOLOGY

Abstracts

Coverage of Indian Scientific periodicals in *Biological Abstracts*—M.K. Thulaja.
(BHU, 1972). 23

Genetics

Changing concepts in genetics since 1965—Sudhir Kumar
(BHU, 1970). 24

Insecticides

Studies on the effects of an insecticide DDT on the biosystem : A trend report, 1977-78--K.C. Mohan.
(University of Mysore, 1979).
(Guide : B. Nagappa). 25

Periodicals

Growth and development of periodical publications in the field of Botany and Zoology—V. Sivaraman.
(University of Delhi, 1974).
(Guide : M.M. Kashyap). 26

Pollution

Environmental pollution due to use of carbamate pesticides and their effect on plants and animals : A trend report, 1977-78—K. C. Ramakrishna Gowda.
(University of Mysore, 1979).
(Guide : B. Nagappa). 27

Legal aspects of environmental pollution : A trend report—S.N. Agrawal.
(INSDOC, 1975).
(Guide : R.K. Khan). 28

Entry No.

BOOK SCIENCE

Abstracting

Abstracting journals in sciences : An analytical and comparative study—M.B. Rama. (University of Mysore, 1982). (Guide : R. Shalini). 29

Abstracting of Ph. D. theses of Economics submitted to the MS University of Baroda during 1951-80—Kautilya H. Shukla. (Vikram University, 1983). (Guide : G.D. Bhargava). 30

Abstracting of Ph.D. theses of Political Science submitted to Punjab University, Chandigarh—Balwinder Singh. (Punjab University, 1982). 31

Analytical study of the coverage, nature of abstracts and indexing of the Indian Science Abstracts, 1969—M.S. Dutta. (INSDOC, 1973). (Guide : B. Guha). 32

Characteristics of the literature of (some specific disciplines) and the coverage of literature in abstracting and indexing services—Onyeadi U. Elizabeth. (Punjab University, 1984). 33

Comparative Study of Biological Abstracts, Chemical Abstracts and Nuclear Abstracts—P. Kumarijyotsna. (Andhra University, 1980). (Guide : B. Vijayalakshmi). 34

Evaluation of Historical Abstracts with special reference to Indian contribution—Sashi Singh. (BHU, 1978). 35

Evaluation of Physical Abstracts with slant to Indian contribution—A.K. Kapoor. (BHU, 1978). 36

Impact of the Rebrativnyi Zhurnal on the use of non-Russian literature by the Soviet scientists as

Entry No.

seen from their citation practices and some characteristics of such citations —T. Karthikeyan. (INSDOC, 1968). (Guide : B. Guha). 37

Indian Science Abstracts, 1972-73—Prasad. (BHU, 1978). 38

Journal literature of sociology : Comprehensive Study Based on Sociological Abstracts—M.P. Paricharak. (INSDOC, 1975). (Guide : T.N. Rajan). 39

Sociological Abstracts : A critical study—K.S. Singh. (BHU, 1978). 40

Tests on abstracting journals : A study of two abstracting journals in Social Sciences—Rajashekaran. (University of Mysore, 1978). (Guide : N.B. Pangannaya). 41

Censorship

Censorship—Paramjit Arora. (BHU, 1971). 42

Censorship—Mohan Singh. (Vikram University, 1976). (Guide : S. Kumar). 43

Children Literature

Children's literature in Malayalam : Proposals for improvement—C.N. Shyamala. (Kerala University, 1982). 44

Study of children's literature, 1950-70—Ram Jita. (Punjab University, 1975). 45

Exhibition

Impact of book exhibition on readers—M.K. Arora. (Punjab University, 1979). 46

Indexing

Alphabetico-subject index of Journal of Indian Management, 1971-75—Gurnam Singh. (Punjab University, 1983). 47

Entry No.

Classified, Chain and KWIC indexing : A Case Study of Library Trends—Pramila Bhatnagar. (University of Rajasthan, 1981). 48

Classified, Chain and KWOC indexing : A Case Study in Indexing Library Resources and Technical Services, V I-20—Purnima Kaushik. (University of Rajasthan, 1981). 49

Classified index of articles in Journal of Indian History, Quarterly Review of Historical Studies, Bengal—Past and Present—Rajender Prasad Mathur. (University of Delhi, 1976). (Guide : M.M. Kashyap). 50

Classified index of articles published in Journal of Indian History in Quarterly Review of Historical Studies, 1975-80—Mahavir Singh. (University of Delhi, 1984). (Guide : K.N. Gupta). 51

Classified index of articles published in Library Science with Slant to Documentation—P.C. Thomas. (University of Delhi, 1974). (Guide : M.M. Kashyap). 52

Conventional Methods of Indexing—Gita Bajpai. (University of Rajasthan, 1978). 53

Cumulative Index of Annals of Library Science and Documentation, 1954-79—Vinod Datta. (Vikram University, 1981). (Guide : S. S. Agrawal). 54

Cumulative Index of Herald of Library Science, 1962-82—Vijaysri Agrawal. (Vikram University, 1983). (Guide : S.S. Agrawal). 55

Cumulative Index of Nucleus Journal, V 1 to 20 : A Study—D.V. Kothari. (University of Rajasthan, 1980). 56

Cumulative Index to Annals of Library Science and Annals of Library Science and Documentation—

Entry No.

Parmanand Sharma.
(University of Delhi, 1974).
(Guide : M.M. Kashyap). 57

Development of the Chain Procedure and its influence on BTI, SLIC and PRECIS—S.S. Puranik.
(INSDOC, 1972).
(Guide : T.N. Rajan). 58

Evaluation of Book Indexes—K.A. Radhakrishna.
(University of Mysore, 1979).
(Guide : N.B. Pangannaya.) 59

Hierarchical, Chain and KWIC indexing : A case study with an index to Iaslic Bulletin—Veena Beguhotta.
(University of Rajasthan, 1981). 60

Indian Press Index : Procedure Manual—Ramesh Chandra Gupta.
(University of Delhi, 1973).
(Guide : M.M. Kashyap). 61

Indexing Methodology—M. Rajbee.
(BHU, 1968). 62

Indexing Methods : Non-conventional—Guruswamy Naidu.
(BHU, 1970). 63

Non-conventional methods of indexing—B.K. Goil.
(University of Rajasthan, 1978). 64

State-of-art report—Rajan.
(University of Delhi, 1983).
(Guide : V.K. Sundaram). 65

Indexing and Abstracting

Comparative analysis of the indexing abstracting and periodicals in the field of Endocrinology—A.D. Kumari Chandra.
(University of Madras, 1983). 66

Comparative analysis of the indexing and abstracting periodicals in the field of Laser Technology—Rohini Vythilingam.
(University of Madras, 1983). 67

Entry No.

Evaluation of indexing and abstracting services in Chemistry—A.R. Saxena. (University of Delhi, 1981). (Guide : J. L. Sardana). 68

Evaluation of indexing and abstracting services in Humanities—R. Sharma. (University of Delhi, 1980). (Guide : K.N. Gupta). 69

Evaluation of indexing and abstracting services in India—R.N. Kaul. (University of Delhi, 1979). (Guide : K.N. Gupta). 70

Evaluation of indexing and abstracting services in Medical Sciences—Sunita. (University of Delhi, 1981). (Guide : M.M. Kashyap). 71

Evaluation of indexing and abstracting services in Physical Sciences—Pavan Arora. (University of Delhi, 1980). (Guide : Krishan Kumar). 72

Evaluation of indexing and abstracting services in Social Sciences in India—Sukhi Ram Bhagat. (University of Delhi, 1974). (Guide : P.B. Mangla). 73

Evaluation of indexing and abstracting services in Social Sciences—V. Rastogi. (University of Delhi, 1981). (Guide : J.L. Sardana). 74

Indexing and abstracting services in India : A literature survey—Sushma Kanungo. (Vikram University, 1981). (Guide : S.S. Agrawal). 75

Indexing and abstracting services in the field of Social, Sciences in India—A.S. Chandel. (BHU, 1974). 76

Indexing and abstracting services of Biological Sciences—Vinay Kumar Singh. (BHU, 1979). 77

Entry No.

Study of indexes of abstracting/indexing services in Science and Technology—A.R. Chakravarty.
(INSDOC, 1975).
(Guide : B. Guha). 78

Study of indexing and abstracting services in Science and Technology with special reference to Physics and Medicine—Sheela V. Paranjpe.
(INSDOC, 1971).
(Guide : T.N. Rajan). 79

Indexing—Citation Index

Citation indexing and literature search through Science Citation Index—J.S. Ghosh.
(INSDOC, 1967).
(Guide : B. Guha). 80

Efficacy of the Science Citation Index for Information Retrieval—D.V. Deshpande.
(INSDOC, 1969).
(Guide : B. Guha). 81

Study on the value of a Citation Index to single periodical—A.K. Ghosh.
(INSDOC, 1970).
(Guide : B. Guha). 82

Indexing—Coordinate Index

Coordinate indexing : A solution to the problem of Information, Storage and Retrieval in Petroleum Technology—B. Garudadwajan.
(INSDOC, 1965).
(Guide : T.N. Rajan). 83

Coordinate indexing, an experiment—M.S. Nomani.
(INSDOC, 1967).
(Guide : T.N. Rajan). 84

Experimental studies on coordinate indexing for organising information on radio communication—Ambrish Kumar.
(INSDOC, 1966).
(Guide : T.N. Rajan). 85

Entry No.

Indexing—POPSI

Chain indexing and POPSI : A case study in indexing periodical literature—B.P. Chauhan.
(University of Rajasthan, 1979). 86

Pilot study of the application of POPSI in a specialized area of Chemistry—R. Jeyabalan.
(Kamaraj University, 1981).
(Guide : D. Chandran). 87

Indexing—Subject Index

Developments and trends in subject indexing since 1960—A.K. Verma.
(BHU, 1980). 88

Development of various subject indexing techniques and their comparative evaluation—A.K. Anand.
(University of Delhi, 1968).
(Guide : P.B. Mangla). 89

Study of the subject indexes of two abstracting services —R.K. Verma.
(INSDOC, 1966).
(Guide : A.K. Dasgupta). 90

Subject indexes : An evaluation—T.R. Mahajan.
(INSDOC, 1967).
(Guide : S. Dutta). 91

Thesaurus

Concept interlinking in coal carbonization : A thesaurus—P. Sahi.
(INSDOC, 1976).
(Guide : S. Rangarajarao). 92

Explosives at War : A thesaurofacet—M.G. Joshi.
(INSDOC, 1975). 93

Thesaurus for a micro subject : Fisheries—K. Kanakasabapati.
(Kamaraj University, 1982).
(Guide : R. Paul Mohan Roy). 94

Entry No.

Thesaurus of mineralogical terms—Srikrishan Kumar.
(INSDOC, 1967).
(Guide : A.S. Raizada). 95

Thesaurus of mining and allied terms—S.K. Gupta.
(INSDOC, 1975).
(Guide : T.N. Rajan). 96

Thesaurus on missile systems—U.R. Sharma.
(INSDOC, 1973).
(Guide : V.B. Tawaklay). 97

BOTANY

Ecology

Trends in pollination ecology—V. Balarami Reddy.
(Andhra University, 1981).
(Guide : B. Vijayalakshmi). 98

Medicine plants

Guide to Indian medicinal plants—Kuldip Chand.
(INSDOC, 1976).
(Guide : B. Guha). 99

Periodicals

Growth of periodical literature in Botany, 1966-75—U.V. Lakshmi.
(University of Delhi, 1979).
(Guide : J.L. Sardana). 100

Periodicals in the field of Botany in Delhi University Library System : A user's survey—H.S. Datta.
(University of Delhi, 1979).
(Guide : Krishan Kumar). 101

Physiology

Plant physiology in India since 1960—N. Laxmanrao.
(BHU, 1971). 102

Effects of sulphur dioxide pollution on plants, 1970-81—K. Srutakeerthi.
(Andhra University, 1981).
(Guide : B. Vijayalakshmi). 103

Entry No.

Taxonomy

Analytical approach to plant taxonomy—
S.K. Banerjee.
(Burdwan University, 1981). 104

CHEMISTRY

Biochemistry

Biochemical research in India : A bibliometric study—
Rajish Singh Rathore.
(BHU, 1979). 105

Biochemistry : Literature survey and trend—
B.L. Chicken.
(BHU, 1966). 106

Chromatography

Advances in chromatography—Vijayasudha.
(Andhra University, 1981).
(Guide : P. Somaraju). 107

Desalination

Bibliographical essay on desalination of salt water—
J.N. Pathak.
(INSDOC, 1967).
(Guide : R. Satyanarayana). 108

Immuno-chemistry

Coverage of literature in the field of immuno-chemistry with relevance to Chemical Abstract's study and its comprehensiveness—H.N. Manjunath.
(Bangalore University, 1978). 109

Index

Cumulative Index of Indian Journal of Chemistry : Section A—Akanksha Nigam.
(Vikram University, 1983).
(Guide : S.S. Agrawal). 110

Entry No.

Literature

Operational research study of the rate of decay of chemical literature : A pilot study on determination of retention period of a periodical—Syed Sirajul Hussain.
(INSDOC, 1965).
(Guide : S. Parthasarathy). 111

Physical Chemistry

Physical Chemistry in India, 1974-78 : A bibliometric study—Rajanikant Shrivastava.
(BHU, 1979). 112

Text books

Evaluation of textbook collections in Chemistry for undergraduate and post-graduate students in three college libraries—Hindu, Ramjas and Kirorimal—Banbarilal.
(University of Delhi, 1981).
(Guide : Krishan Kumar). 113

Evaluation of textbooks in Chemistry in selected libraries of Delhi University Campus Colleges—S.D. Panwar.
(University of Delhi, 1979).
(Guide : J.L. Sardana). 114

ECONOMICS

Agriculture

Agricultural economics—N.H. Pawar.
(BHU, 1968). 115

Study of agricultural economics from American and Indian angles—S.K. Musib.
(Burdwan University, 1981). 116

Banking

Bank nationalisation in India : A literature survey—N.G. Satish.

Entry No.

(University of Mysore, 1976).
(Guide : H.A. Khan). 117

Banks and banking—A.R. Singh.
(BHU, 1968). 118

Bibliography

Post Keynesian literature in economics : A survey—Meena Walia.
(Punjab University, 1971). 119

Business Management

Business Management—S.N. Singh.
(BHU, 1966). 120

Communism

Communism—R.S. Sharma.
(BHU, 1967). 121

Development

Economics of growth—M.P. Singh.
(BHU, 1968). 122

Entrepreneurship

Pre-investment information requirements of small entrepreneurs—M. Ishwara Bhat.
(Bangalore University, 1976). 123

Imports

Indian import policy, 1950-70—R.S. Tiwari.
(BHU, 1971). 124

Industry

Directory of glass and ceramic industry in India—A.K. Roy.
(INSDOC, 1972).
(Guide : B.M. Bishni). 125

Dyestuff industry in India : A review—S. Deshmukh.
(INSDOC, 1979).
(Guides : J.B. Subramaniam and C. Spurgen. 126

Entry No.

Industrial economics—N.B. Pangannaya.
(BHU, 1968). 127

Information sources on engineering industry—
S. Senguttuvan.
(INSDOC, 1978).
(Guide : J.B. Subramaniam). 128

Iron and steel industry in India : A survey—
P.K. Chaudhury.
(INSDOC, 1966).
(Guide : T.N. Rajan). 129

Perspective and information sources on Indian chemical industry—K.S. Reddy.
(INSDOC, 1978).
(Guide : S. Dutta). 130

Processed food industries in India—R. Veeraraghavan.
(INSDOC, 1968).
(Guide : B. Guha). 131

Trend report on operations research for industry and management—S.N. Vig.
(INSDOC, 1970).
(Guide : Dhanpat Rai) 132

Trend report on synthetic rubber industry in India—
J. Shriram.
(INSDOC, 1975).
(Guides : T.N. Rajan and B. Guha). 133

Industry—Smallscale

Assistance programmes for smallscale industry in India : Information sources—S.R. Nagalla.
(INSDOC, 1973).
(Guide : T.N. Rajan). 134

Information for small industry : A survey—
B.S. Sudhakararao.
(INSDOC, 1979).
(Guide : J.B. Subramaniam). 135

Smallscale industries in India—Sreenivasa Sastry.
(BHU, 1976). 136

Entry No.

Smallscale industries in India—P.C. Tiwari. (BHU, 1972). 137

Industry—Thesaurus

Thesaurus of Small industry development terms for SENDOC : A report and micro-thesaurus—R. Kalavati. (INSDOC, 1979). (Guide : L.J. Haravu). 138

Labour

Labour movement in India since independence—Pushpa Dhyani. (BHU, 1971). 139

Literature

Growth and development of literature on economic planning in India since 1961 with special reference to the role of different institutions—G.C. Bansal. (University of Delhi, 1968). (Guide : P.B. Mangla). 140

Growth and development of periodical literature in India in the field of economics with special referrence to post-independence period—Ajit Kumar Talukdar. (University of Delhi, 1974). (Guide : P.D. Mangla). 141

Management

Managerial satisfaction of needs—R.V. Gopalarao. (Andhra University, 1981). (Guide : P. Somaraju). 142

Personnel Management

Human relations : A behavioural approach to personnel management—J. Muralidhar. (Andhra University, 1980). (Guide : K. Sarada). 143

Entry No.

Personnel management : A thesaurus—
C.R. Madhusudanrao.
(University of Mysore, 1982).
(Guide : B. Nagappa). 144

Technical manpower of India : A survey of literature
—C.R.S. Rao.
(INSDOC, 1969).
(Guide : S. Parthasarathy). 145

Public Sector, India

Managerial aspects of public enterprises in India : A
bibliographical survey—V.K. Vedapuri.
(INSDOC, 1969).
(Guide : T.N. Rajan). 146

Public sector undertaking in India--G. Suryarao.
(Andhra University, 1981).
(Guide : G.V.S.L.N. Raju). 147

Public undertakings in India since 1950—
S.P. Mukherjee.
(BHU). 148

Socialism

Socialism—J.S. Tiwana.
(BHU, 1966). 149

Socialism—M.L. Pasrija.
(BHU, 1968). 150

Textbooks

Evaluation of the textbooks collection in economics
and sociology at post-graduate level in Delhi
School of Economics Library (Rattan Tata Library)
—R.L. Sehgal.
(University of Delhi, 1981).
(Guide : K.N. Gupta). 151

Transport

Economics of road transport in India : A trend report,
1970-73—S. Kasiviswanatham.

Entry No.

(INSDOC, 1973).
(Guide : M.C. Raghawan). 152

Organisation of railways in India—B.K. Singh.
(BHU, 1972). 153

Railway transportation in India—C.K. Sharma.
(BHU, 1970). 154

EDUCATION

Adult Education

Adult education—C.C. Bhandari.
(BHU, 1967). 155

Role of Karnataka State Adult Education Council in the development of rural libraries : A case study of Mysore taluk—Manorama Mishra.
(University of Mysore, 1978).
(Guide : H.A. Khan). 156

Role of libraries in National Adult Education Programme (NAEP) : Literature survey—Ratan Babu Kamtamnani.
(University of Rajasthan, 1980). 157

Role of public libraries in adult education—Suraj Prakash.
(Punjab University, 1979). 158

Role of public libraries in adult education in U.S.A., U.K. and India—S.Y. Ismail.
(University of Delhi, 1981).
(Guide : D.S. Agrawal). 159

Associate learning

Paired associate learning—K. Ranirao.
(Andhra University, 1980). 160

Audio-Visual

Audio-visual education—M.S. Subramaniam.
(BHU, 1970). 161

Bibliography

Classified bibliography of secondary education in

Entry No.

India : 1950-76—Annie Mathew.
(University of Delhi, 1977).
(Guide : J.L. Sardana). 162

Classified bibliography on higher education in India, 1950-75—Mathuri Devi.
(University of Delhi, 1977).
(Guide : J.L. Sardana). 163

Committees and Commissions

Indian education : Reports of the Committees and Commissions—V.N. Kusuma.
(INSDOC, 1969).
(Guide : A.K. Dasgupta). 164

Extracurricular activities

Place of extracurricular reading among extracurricular activities in post-graduate students of men's hostel, Manasagangotri, Mysore—T.D. Kemparaju.
(University of Mysore, 1979).
(Guide : H.A. Khan). 165

India

Economics of education in India—S. Indira.
(Andhra University, 1980).
(Guide : B. Vijayalakshmi). 166

Education in India—A.A.N. Raju.
(BHU. 1966). 167

Reforms in education in India, 1947-70 : A literature survey—Ved Prakash Gupta.
(Punjab University, 1975). 168

Study of the growth and development of university education in India since 1850 with critical evaluation of the sources—K.A. Seethalakshmi
(University of Delhi, 1968).
(Guide : K.N. Gupta). 169

Institutions

Role of NCERT in the field of education—

Entry No.

Shailbala.
(Punjab University, 1980). 170

Planning

Educational planning in India, 1966-70—D.R. Kanwal.
(BHU, 1975). 171

Reading habits

Reading habits of users in Indore University Library —Umesh Kulkarni.
(Vikram University, 1981).
(Guide : S.S. Agrawal). 172

Survey of reading habits—P.K. Jayaswal.
(BHU, 1971). 173

Reading habits—Children

Children's reading habits : A case study of Shri Venkateswara Bala Kuteer, Guntur—K.S. Sarma.
(Andhra University, 1981).
(Guide : P. Somaraju). 174

Reading habits—Executives

Reading habits of executives in the pharmaceutical industry in the city of Bombay and their use of information sources—R. Kuvalekar.
(Bombay University, 1977). 175

Reading habits—Females

Reading habits among girls of University of Rajasthan Library System : A field survey—Hemlata Gupta.
(University of Rajasthan, 1981). 176

Reading habits of women of Chandigarh : A survey —Shashi Anand.
(Punjab University, 1983). 177

Survey of reading habits of women users in Ujjain city —Seema Mathur.
(Vikram University, 1983).
(Guide : S.S. Agrawal). 178

Entry No.

Reading habits—Library staff

Survey of reading habits of library professionals in college and university libraries in Pune—N.S. Karandikar.
(Poona University, 1980).
(Guide : T.H. Lagu). 179

Reading habits—Research scholars

Reading habits of research scholars and post-graduate students in university library and college libraries of Indore city—T.S. Rathor.
(Vikram University, 1980).
(Guide : G.D. Bhargava). 180

Reading habits of social science research scholars of the Benares Hindu University—S.M. Tripathi.
(BHU, 1978). 181

Reading habits—Students

Extracurricular reading habits of the students of the undergraduate classes of science faculty, BHU. —J.R. Ramamurthy.
(BHU, 1971). 182

Reading habits among secondary school children in south Madras : A survey—Suseela Ganesan.
(University of Madras, 1981). 183

Reading habits and information needs of students of the faculty of Arts, Punjab University : A survey —Ramji Dass.
(Punjab University, 1973). 184

Reading habits of college students : A study—A.R. Dharwadkar.
(Dharwar University, 1981).
(Guide : Kumbhar). 185

Reading habits of post-graduate students of Gulbarga University : A survey—D.V. Biradar.
(Dharwar University, 1982).
(Guide : Kumbhar). 186

Reading habits of post-graduate students of Osmania

Entry No.

University, Hyderabad : A survey—
(Dharwar University, 1977).
(Guide : Kumbhar). 187

Reading habits of post-SSLC and undergraduate students of Basaveshwar Arts College, Bagalkot : A study—N.C. Hiremath.
(Dharwar University, 1980).
(Guide : Kumbhar). 188

Reading habits of Pre-University Course students —P.C. Tiwari.
(BHU, 1971). 189

Reading habits of the secondary school students in Jaipur : A field survey—Indu Agrawal.
(University of Rajasthan, 1979). 190

Reading habits of undergraduates in twentyfive colleges in the city of Bombay—S.R. Gandule.
(Bombay University, 1970). 191

Study of reading interests and habits of college students in an urban and rural setting : A comparative study—H.S. Shanthalakshamma.
(Bangalore University, 1979). 192

Survey of the reading habits of students in the secondary schools in Kerala with special reference to educational district, Trivandrum —G. Devarajan.
(University of Madras, 1980). 193

Reading habits—Teachers

Reading habits of teachers, research scholars and post-graduate students of K.S. Saket P.G. College, Avadh University—A. Yadav.
(BHU, 1978). 194

Reading habits of the faculty in sciences : A case study of Punjab University, Chandigarh —Shashiprabha.
(Punjab University, 1984). 195

Reading habits of the faculty in social sciences : A case study of Punjab University, Chandigarh

Entry No.

—Harleen.
(Punjab University, 1984). 196

University education

Establishment of documentation services in an Indian university—Parmod Kumar Goyal.
(Punjab University, 1981). 197

ENGINEERING

Aeronautics

Aerospace technical reports : Problems and Prospects —C.D. Lailambika Amma.
(Kerala University, 1980). 198

Guide to source of information in aeronautical sciences and engineering—M.N. Seetharaman.
(INSDOC, 1977).
(Guide : S. Parthasarathy). 199

Role of titanium in aerospace technology : A report —D.M. Nair.
(INSDOC, 1973).
(Guide : T.K.G. Namboodhiri). 200

Buildings

Building science research in India : A quantitative study of the literature—S.C. Sinha.
(INSDOC, 1979).
(Guides : T.N. Rajan and Arunachalam). 201

Guide to information sources in building science —Kuldip Kaur.
(INSDOC, 1970).
(Guide : K.S. Srinivasan). 202

Trend report on building materials with special reference to plastics, 1961-65—S. Srinivasan.
(INSDOC, 1966).
(Guide : S. Parthasarathy). 203

Trend report on prefabrication as applied to buildings, 1970-75—Inamul Haq.

Entry No.

(INSDOC, 1976).
(Guide : S. Srinivasan). 204

Computers

Biblioprofile on mini-computers with an indication of recent trends—S. Saradambal.
(Bangalore University, 1978). 205

Personnel in the computer field : Their needs and sources of information—A.M. Nichani.
(SNDT Wowen's University, 1981). 206

Drawings

Engineering drawings and their organisation in industrial complex—D.K. Mahajan.
(INSDOC, 1975)
(Guide : T.N. Rajan). 207

Electric circuits

Analysis of literature on integrated circuits with indications of recent development—V.G. Talwar.
(Bangalore University, 1978). 208

Electronics

Electronics in India : A profile for the period 1965-70 —H.S.D. Khatri.
(INSDOC, 1974).
(Guide : A.S. Raizada). 209

Microelectronics : A trend report, 1972-74 —K. Ravindra.
(University of Mysore, 1975).
(Guide : T.V. Subramaniam). 210

Usage pattern of literature on electronics in India for the period 1965-69—Chandraprakash.
(INSDOC, 1970).
(Guide : A.S. Raizada). 211

Mechanical

Remotely piloted vehicles : A trend report—Izzath

Entry No.

Jehan Begum.
(INSDOC, 1975).
(Guides : A. Neelameghan and T. Varghese). 212

Radar

Trend in the development of military and civilian applications of radar during the years 1961-65 —Balaram.
(INSDOC, 1966).
(Guide : D.A. Tellis). 213

Semi conductors

Semi conductor devices : A trend report for the period 1961-64—V.K. Gupta.
(INSDOC, 1965).
(Guide : G.K. Arora). 214

Solar energy

Analysis of solar energy research in USSR : A citation study—B.M. Gupta.
(INSDOC, 1976).
(Guide : B. Guha). 215

Structural engineering

Structural engineering research in India, 1965-72 —N. Jayaraman.
(INSDOC, 1972).
(Guide : T.S. Rajagopalan). 216

Telecommunication

Bibliographic organisation in telecommunication engineering—Saghir Hasan.
(INSDOC, 1967).
(Guide : B. Guha). 217

Role of telecommunication in information and communication—S.C. Banerjee.
(INSDOC, 1975).
(Guide : V. Topa). 218

Entry No.

Television

Television as a mass media of communication : An analysis—A. Amudhavalli.
(University of Madras, 1981). 219

Television : social impact on audience—C. Sasikala.
(Andhra University, 1981).
(Guide : K. Sarada). 220

FINE ARTS

Architecture—College library buildings

Critical appraisal of the Hindu College Library and Indraprastha College for Women library buildings —R.S. Dabas.
(University of Delhi, 1974).
(Guide : P.B. Mangla). 221

Recently constructed college library buildings : An evaluative study—Poonam Sardana.
(University of Delhi, 1978).
(Guide : Krishan Kumar). 222

Architecture—Research library buildings

Critical appraisal of two Library buildings : Indian Institute of Public Administration and Rattan Tata Library—V.N. Mittangi.
(University of Delhi, 1974).
(Guide : M.M. Kashyap). 223

Evaluation of library buildings of Indian Agricultural Research Institute and N.M. Library—Satyapal Singh.
(University of Delhi, 1974).
(Guide : M.M. Kashyap). 224

Architecture—University library buildings

Library buildings of Vikram and Indore Universities : A comparison—P.K. Vyas.
(Vikram University, 1980).
(Guide : S. Kumar). 225

Entry No.

University library buildings with special reference to India: Literature survey—Sandhya Sharma. (University of Rajasthan, 1980). 226

University library buildings of Varanasi—S.N. Khiste. (BHU, 1968). 227

Museology

Museology in relation to education—Santi Das. (BHU, 1974). 228

Music

Prominent composers of Carnatic Music : A bibliographical study—K.V. Sandhyakumari. (University of Mysore, 1977). (Guide : T.V. Subramanyam). 229

Painting

Kangra miniature paintings : History and development —L.P. Sharma. (BHU, 1971). 230

GENERALIA

American studies

American studies—S.K. Chatterji. (Burdwan University, 1980). 231

Bangladesh

Development studies in Bangladesh in the context of the Devsis plan—M.D. Serajul Haque. (INSDOC, 1976). (Guide : B. Guha). 232

Himachal Pradesh

Himachal Pradesh : A select annotated bibliography —Ramesh Chandra Datta. (Punjab University, 1980). 233

Entry No.

Indology

Indian statistical sources : An annotated guide—
T.D. Ghuliani
(INSDOC, 1973).
(Guide : B. Guha). 234

Indological studies abroad—D.D. Kapil.
(BHU, 1967). 235

Indological studies in India, 1960-66—R.S. Sharma.
(BHU, 1970). 236

Sources of statistical information of India—
T.B. Chitale.
(Bombay University, 1972). 237

Bibliography

Jayaprakash Narain—Ramesh Phookan.
(BHU, 1973). 238

Mahatma Gandhi : A bibliography, 1970-80—
G.N. Kalbhor.
(Vikram University, 1982).
(Guide : G. D. Bhargava). 239

Planning, India

Indian planning since independence—
N. Guruswamy Naidu.
(BHU, 1970). 240

Third Five-Year Plan of India—Y.P. Dubey.
(BHU, 1968). 241

Who is Who

Who is Who of the important working leaders—
Jyoti Surana.
(University of Rajasthan, 1981). 242

Who is Who of the important working leaders
(Jaipur)—Janak Kharbanda.
(University of Rajasthan, 1981). 243

GENERALIA BIBLIOGRAPHY

Bibliography—C.L. Sharma.
(University of Rajasthan, 1975). 244

Entry No.

Development of bibliography and bibliographical services : A trend report—M.S. Muthuvelu. (Kamaraj University, 1981). (Guide : R. Paulmohan Roy). 245

Document bibliography—A. Tejomurty. (Vikram University, 1976). (Guide : S.S. Agrawal). 246

Literature published on handicapped : A select annotated bibliography—Hari Om Prakash. (Punjab University, 1980). 247

Recent trends in the development of standards for bibliography description—M.V. Hithaishini. (Bangalore University, 1975). 248

Servants of the People Society and its literature : A general survey—Devinder Kaur. (Punjab University, 1978). 249

Books

Annotated bibliography of books on Indian History and Politics in English language published outside India—M.M. Ismail. (University of Delhi, 1981). (Guide : P.B.Mangla). 250

Children's books in Tamil, 1963-82 : An analysis—M. Nagarajan. (University of Madras, 1983). 251

Retrospective bibliographical control of Tamil books with special reference to "The Madras State Tamil Bibliography" (1867-1935) : An evaluation—T.C. Chandrababu. (University of Madras, 1979). 252

Contribution

Contribution of H.W. Wilson in the field of bibliography—Rashmi. (Punjab University, 1979). 253

Entry No.

Festschrift

Study of Indian festschriften in English language—
J.B. Jadhav.
(INSDOC, 1970).
(Guide : T.N. Rajan). 254

India

Bibliographical literature in India : A survey and trend, 1967-76.
(BHU, 1979). 255

Classified annotated bibliography of 20 point economic programme in India—Bhadrakanta Borah.
(University of Delhi, 1977).
(Guide : M.M. Kashyap). 256

Delhi : A select classified and annotated bibliography—Vandana Dhakar.
(University of Delhi, 1978).
(Guide : P.B. Mangla). 257

Evaluation of selected bibliographical services in bibliographical sciences in India, UK, USA—A.V. Vijayalakshmi.
(University of Delhi, 1980).
(Guide : J.L. Sardana). 258

Revolt of 1857 : An evaluation of selected printed sources—Noor-ul Hassan Khan.
(University of Delhi, 1968).
(Guide : P.B. Mangla). 259

Languages—English

Indian writings in English—J.R. Ramamurthy.
(BHU, 1971). 260

Languages—Gujarati

Bibliographical survey and control of Gujarati publications—K.G. Vaidya.
(Bombay University, 1973). 261

Entry No.

Languages—Hindi

Bibliography of curricular and cocurricular Hindi books in social sciences—Veena Ahuja.
(University of Delhi, 1970).
(Guide : M.M. Kashyap). 262

Bibliography of curricular and cocurricular Hindi books of university level in social sciences—Sumitra Aggarwal.
(University of Delhi, 1970).
(Guide : M.M. Kashyap). 263

Bibliography of curricular and cocurricular university level Hindi books in social sciences—V.K. Chugh.
(University of Delhi, 1970).
(Guide : M.M. Kashyap). 264

Classified bibliography of articles in Hindi language and literature, 1970-77—Ranjana Kakkar.
(University of Delhi, 1977).
(Guide : D.S. Aggarwal). 265

Classified bibliography of articles in Hindi language and literature, 1977-83—Brijbala.
(University of Delhi, 1984).
(Guide : C.P. Vashishth). 266

Languages—Kannada

Jaina literature in Kannada : A bibliography—P.Y. Rajendrakumar.
(University of Mysore, 1974).
(Guide : B. Nagappa). 267

Languages—Malayalam

Scheme for the bibliographic control of Malayalam literature with special reference to published classics—P. Parameswaran.
(University of Madras, 1978). 268

Languages—Marathi

Bibliographical control of Marathi publications : A

Entry No.

critical survey—Shanta Sharma.
(Poona University, 1981).
(Guide : M.P. Pethe). 269

Manuscripts

Critical evaluation of the bibliographical sources for Sanskrit manuscripts—Pushpalata Taneja.
(University of Delhi, 1968).
(Guide : K.N. Gupta). 270

Microforms

Microforms, their use in research—V.N. Misra.
(INSDOC, 1966).
(Guide : N.R.R. Chari). 271

Patents

Bibliographical control and use of patents in research libraries—I.R.A. Roy.
(SNDT Women's University, 1980). 272

Bibliographical control of patent literature—Aref Kamal Awad.
University of Delhi, 1975).
(Guide : M.M. Kashyap). 273

Growth of patents in India after 1947—Mohinder Prakash Khanna.
(INSDOC, 1968).
(Guide : S. Dutta). 274

Organisation of patent literature as a potential source of information for applied research—Budhendu Bijoy Misra.
(INSDOC, 1967).
(Guide : S. Dutta). 275

Patent information : characteristics and a system for India—Ashok Kumar Jain.
(Punjab University, 1981). 276

Periodicals

Bibliographical control of periodicals and serials with

Entry No.

special reference to India—Arunprabha.
(Punjab University, 1981). 277

Evolution of Indian periodical literature : A study upto 1947—Balkrishan Sharma.
(Punjab University, 1972). 278

Growth and development of periodical publications in Tamil language—K. Perumalsamy.
(Kamaraj University, 1980).
(Guides : A. Tirumalaimuthusamy and D.B. Krishnarao). 279

Origin and development of periodical literature in English language in India upto 1947 : A survey—Rameshpal Arora.
(Punjab University, 1979). 280

Organisation and bibliographical control of periodical literature in scientific libraries (with special reference to the Indian Institute of Science Library, Bangalore)—G.B. Nadgir.
(Bombay University, 1981). 281

Ranking of library science periodicals on the basis of citation analysis—Pushplata Malik.
(University of Delhi, 1976).
(Guide : Krishna Kumar). 282

Quantitative analysis of Indian publications, 1960-64—Pushpa P. Butani.
(INSDOC, 1966).
(Guide : A. K. Dasgupta). 283

Reference books

Annotated bibliography of reference books published in India in medical sciences from 1950-70—C.P.M. Koya.
(University of Delhi, 1971).
(Guide : B.V.R. Rao). 284

Annotated bibliography of selected reference books in biology, agriculture and animal sciences published in India with a brief survey of reference books—B.L. Kachru.

Entry No.

(University of Delhi, 1970).
(Guide : M.M. Kashyap). 285

Annotated bibliography of selected reference books in physical sciences, engineering and technology and medical sciences published in India : brief survey of reference books—K.S. Raghavan.
(University of Delhi, 1970).
(Guide : M.M. Kashyap). 286

Bibliography of reference books published in India—D.V. Rawal.
(University of Delhi, 1971).
(Guide : B.V.R. Rao). 287

Bibliography of reference material published in biological sciences in India in English from 1950-70—T.A.V. Murthy.
(University of Delhi, 1970).
(Guide : B.V.R. Rao). 288

Bibliography of selected reference tools on economics published in India—Balraj Kumar Suri.
(University of Delhi, 1971).
(Guide : K.N. Gupta). 289

Evaluation of reference and bibliographical sources in Sanskrit literature—Minakshi Puri.
(University of Delhi, 1968).
(Guide : D.S. Aggarwal). 290

Evaluation of selected Indian reference books in natural sciences—K. Navlani.
(University of Delhi, 1968).
(Guide : Krishan Kumar). 291

Evaluation of selected reference tools in economics published in India—Veena Chopra.
(University of Delhi, 1968).
(Guide : Krishan Kumar). 292

Evaluation of selected reference tools in political science and law published in India—Usha Gulati.
(University of Delhi, 1971).
(Guide : B.V.R. Rao). 293

Evaluation of selected reference works and biblio-

Entry No.

graphical sources in Hindi—Maya Gupta.
(University of Delhi, 1968).
(Guide : D.S. Aggarwal). 294

Indian reference books in physical sciences : An annotated bibliography of books in English published between 1950-70—H.M.K. Moodgil.
(Uuiversity of Delhi, 1971). 295

Reference literature in Malayalam : A chronological survey—M. Varghese.
(Kerala University, 1980). 296

Select bibliography of reference books published in India in History—K. Lazarus.
(University of Delhi, 1971).
(Guide : B.V.R. Rao). 297

Selective bibliography of reference sources published in India in agricultural sciences during 1950-70—Bhagwan Dass.
(University of Delhi, 1971).
(Guide : B.V.R. Rao). 298

Reports

Annotated and classified bibliography of project reports submitted in Library Science Department —Margret M. Mulwa.
(University of Delhi, 1983).
(Guide : C.P. Vashishth). 299

Reports literature : Characteristics, features, problems and bibliographical control—Sukhraj Rosha.
(Punjab University, 1981). 300

Theses

Annotated and classified bibliography of Ph. D. theses submitted to Delhi University in Arabic, Persian and Urdu—Sadia Praveen.
(University of Delhi, 1980).
(Guide : C.P. Vashishth). 301

Annotated and classified bibliography of Ph. D. theses submitted to Delhi University in biological

Entry No.

sciences—Veena Saraf.
(University of Delhi, 1978).
(Guide : P.B. Mangla). 302

Annotated and classified bibliography of Ph. D. theses submitted to Delhi University in Economics and Sociology—Kamlesh Kakhar.
(University of Delhi, 1978).
(Guide : C.P. Vashishth). 303

Annotated and classified bibliography of Ph. D. theses submitted to Delhi University in Hindi literature—Asha Arora.
(University of Delhi, 1980).
(Guide : M.M. Kashyap). 304

Annotated and classified bibliography of Ph. D. theses submitted to Delhi University in History, Political Science and African Studies—Prakriti Ranjan Goswami.
(University of Delhi, 1978).
(Guide : J.L. Sardana). 305

Annotated and classified bibliography of theses submitted to Delhi University in Inorganic and Physical Chemistry during 1968-78—Usha Mujoo.
(University of Delhi, 1980).
(Guide : J.L. Sardana). 306

Annotated and classified bibliography of Ph. D. theses submitted to Delhi University in Organic Chemistry during 1960-76—Manjula Anand.
(University of Delhi, 1978). 307

Annotated and classified bibliography of Ph. D. theses submitted to Delhi University in Sanskrit—Sadhna.
(University of Delhi, 1981).
(Guide : C.P. Vashishth). 308

Annotated and classified bibliography of Ph. D. theses submitted to Delhi University in Sanskrit during 1960-76—Saroj Kumari.
(University of Delhi, 1978).
(Guide : K.N. Gupta). 309

Entry No.

Annotated and classified bibliography of Ph. D. theses submitted to Delhi University in Urdu during 1967-82—Nasreen Begum.
(University of Delhi, 1984).
(Guide : K.N. Gupta). 310

Bibliometric analysis of doctoral dissertations in Chemistry—Thippeswamy.
(University of Mysore, 1983).
(Guide : R. Shalini). 311

M. Phil and Ph. D. dissertations accepted for award by the Himachal Pradesh University, Shimla, between 1974-80 : An annotated bibliography—Ram Prakash Sharma.
(Punjab University, 1981). 312

Theses and dissertations collections in Iraq : A critical appraisal of the problem of organisation and control—Shafiuddin.
(Osmania University, 1982). 313

Translations

Bibliographical control of translations in science and technology—V. Rajalakshmi.
(INSDOC, 1967).
(Guide : T.S. Rajagopalan). 314

Union Catalogue

Union catalogue—U.S. Mishra.
(BHU, 1967). 315

Union catalogue of books published prior to 1920 in the field of social sciences in Hindu College Library and St. Stephen's Library—Sudha Gambhir.
(University of Delhi, 1977).
(Guide : C.P. Vashishth). 316

Union Catalogue—India

Union catalogues of India : An examination and evaluation—D.K. Ahuja.
(University of Delhi, 1976). 317

Entry No.

Union catalogues of serials in India : A survey—Hansraj Chopra.
(Punjab University, 1975). 318

Union catalogues published by INSDOC : An evaluation and examination—Bhavana Shukla.
(University of Delhi, 1979).
(Guide : Krishna Kumar). 319

Union catalogue with special reference to India—M.L. Agrawal.
(University of Rajasthan, 1977). 320

Union Catalogue—Periodicals

Union catalogue of law periodicals in libraries of Delhi—M.K. Bakshi.
(University of Delhi, 1977).
(Guide : M.M. Kashyap). 321

Union catalogue of library science periodical holdings in DUL, JNUL and NSL—R.N. Chopra.
(University of Delhi, 1979).
(Guide : K.N. Gupta). 322

Union catalogue of periodicals in college and university libraries of Gwalior city—Rakesh Srivastava.
(Vikram University, 1982).
(Guide : S.S. Agrawal). 323

Union catalogue of periodicals in college and university libraries of Rewa—Padmaja Thakkar.
(Vikram University, 1983).
(Guide : S.S. Agrawal). 324

Union catalogue of periodicals in Ujjain city—Deepak Saxena.
(Vikram University, 1982).
(Guide : S.S. Agrawal). 325

Union catalogue of science periodicals in Indore city—Nalini Saxena.
(Vikram University, 1982).
(Guide : G.D. Bhargava). 326

Entry No.

GEOGRAPHY

Andhra Pradesh

Regional geography of Andhra Pradesh—
Hemasundara Naidu.
(Andhra University, 1980).
(Guide : G.V.S.L.R. Raju). 327

Bibliography

Bibliography on atmospheric pollution metereology, 1965-70 with author and subject index—
Amarjit Singh.
(INSDOC, 1970).
(Guide : P.S. Harihara Iyer). 328

GEOLOGY

New global tectonics : A review—K.A. Raju
(INSDOC, 1972).
(Guide : C. Subramanyam). 329

Earthquake

Earthquake—Parasnath.
(BHU, 1967). 330

Groundwater

Groundwater—K. Venkatareddy.
(Andhra University, 1980).
(Guide : K. Sarada). 331

Metallurgy

Trend report on researches in non-ferrous extractive metallurgy, 1958-68—R. Chokkaiyan.
(INSDOC, 1969).
(Guide : A.K. Dasgupta). 332

Mining

Trend report on rock mechanics as applied to mining: A bibliographical study, 1968-71—S.K. Roy.

Entry No.

(INSDOC, 1972).
(Guide : A.K. Ghosh). 333

HISTORY

Civil Service, India

Civil services in India : A literature survey—M.S. Garga.
(Punjab University, 1971). 334

Indian Civil Service (from inception to the present day) : A bibliographical study—J.P. Gupta.
(INSDOC, 1970).
(Guide : T.N. Rajan). 335

India

Sources of information in Indian history (British period 1600—1947) : An annotated bibliography—Krishankant Sharma.
(Punjab University, 1976). 336

Kashmir question

Genesis of Kashmir question, 1947-65—R.K. Kour.
(BHU, 1972). 337

Periodicals

Periodical literature : history and problems in library services—P.N. Vohra.
(University of Delhi, 1964). 338

Research methodology

Methodology of historical research in modern India—A. Dasgupta.
(BHU, 1976). 339

Revolt

Revolt of 1857—Paramjit Arora.
(BHU, 1971). 340

Entry No.

JOURNALISM

Journalism in India since independence—
T. Madhusudanrao.
(BHU, 1972). 341

LAW

Bibliography

Bibliography of Indian law—J.E. Chalil.
(Bombay University, 1971). 342

Copyright Act

Origin and development of Copyright Act : A survey throughout world with reference to UK, USA and India—Rajkumar.
(Punjab University, 1981). 343

Hindu law

Hindu law and its statutory changes since 1947—
P. Purkayastha.
(BHU, 1967). 344

Hindu marriage

Hindu marriage—U.S. Misra.
(BHU, 1967). 345

Land reforms

Land reforms in India—Sadhana Sain.
(Burdwan University, 1980). 346

Periodical literature

Growth and development of periodical literature in law in India—Asha Wanchoo.
(University of Delhi, 1976). 347

LIBRARY AND INFORMATION SCIENCE

Academic libraries

Academic libraries in Gwalior city—Lata Vyas.

Entry No.

(Vikram University, 1979).
(Guide : S. Kumar). 348

Academic libraries of Himachal Pradesh : A survey—Kapura Ram.
(Punjab University, 1983). 349

Audio-visual materials in academic libraries in India : A survey—Rita.
(Punjab University, 1983). 350

Growth and development of academic libraries in India after 1947—M.D. Baby.
(University of Delhi, 1974).
(Guide : M.M. Kashyap). 351

Public relation work in academic libraries : A literature survey—S.T. Nigam.
(University of Rajasthan, 1979). 352

University and college libraries—S.S. Panwar.
(University of Rajasthan, 1978). 353

Academic libraries—Acquisition

Acquisition policy in academic libraries of Varanasi—C.R. Karisiddappa.
(BHU, 1971). 354

Procurement of periodical literature in academic libraries : A literature survey—Padma Hukmani.
(University of Rajasthan, 1979). 355

Academic libraries—Book selection

Book selection in academic libraries : A literature survey—R.R. Sharma.
(University of Rajasthan, 1979). 356

Academic libraries—College libraries

College library—Shobha Sharma.
(BHU, 1967). 357

Academic libraries—College libraries
Andhra Pradesh

College libraries in Vijayawada : A study—

Entry No.

D. Vijayasaradhi.
(Andhra University, 1980).
(Guide : K. Siva Reddy). 358

College libraries in Visakhapatnam—R.V. Gopalarao.
(Andhra University, 1981).
(Guide : P. Somaraju). 359

Engineering College library of Andhra University—K. Krishnamurthy.
(Andhra University, 1980).
(Guide : K. Sarada). 360

Junior college libraries in Anantapur district, (AP) : A survey—D. Rajeswari.
(Madras University, 1983). 361

Junior college libraries in Chittoor district (AP) : A survey—B.R. Karunakaran.
(Madras University, 1982). 362

Padmavathi Women's College library, Tirupati : A development plan—N. Varalakshmi.
(Dharwar University, 1978).
(Guide : Kumbhar). 363

Readers service in professional college libraries in Hyderabad : A survey—V. Urmila.
(Osmania University, 1982). 364

Study of library facilities in selected colleges in Tirupati—B. Rameshbabu.
(University of Mysore, 1979).
(Guide : N.B. Pangannaya). 365

Study of the working of campus and constituent college libraries of Osmania University—Anagha Inamdar.
(Osmania University, 1982). 366

Survey of library facilities in degree colleges in Guntur district (AP)—S. Satyanarayana.
(Madras University, 1983). 367

Academic libraries—College libraries, Delhi

Acquisition policy and procedures followed by the libraries of Delhi University Campus Colleges—

Entry No.

K.S. Rao.
(Delhi University, 1978).
(Guide : Krishan Kumar). 368

Comparison and evaluation of Political Science collection and their use in Ramjas and Indraprastha College libraries—Nasreen Taj Qureshi.
(University of Delhi, 1978).
(Guide : V.K. Sundaram). 369

Comparison and evaluation of Sanskrit collections and their use in St. Stephen's and Hindu College libraries—Lata Tyagi.
(University of Delhi, 1978).
(Guide : M.M. Kashyap). 370

Critical appraisal of the use of services of Rajdhani College, Shivaji College libraries—M.M. Khan.
(University of Delhi, 1980).
(Guide : Krishan Kumar). 371

Critical evaluation of reference collection in the field of English literature in campus colleges of the University of Delhi—Sreekantan Nair.
(University of Delhi, 1976).
(Guide : M.M. Kashyap). 372

Evaluation and use of book collection in Chemistry in Hansraj College and Hindu College libraries—S.M. Shafi.
(University of Delhi, 1978).
(Guide : K.N. Gupta). 373

Evaluation and use of book collection in History in the Hindu College and Hansraj College libraries—Ratan Singh Saini.
(University of Delhi, 1978).
(Guide : M.M. Kashyap). 374

Evaluation and use of books in Physics in selected libraries of the Delhi University Campus Colleges —V. Pullareddy.
(University of Delhi, 1978).
(Guide : J.L. Sardana). 375

Evaluation and use of English textbook collection in

Entry No.

the libraries of Daulat Ram College and Miranda House in respect of M.A. (English) course of the University of Delhi—N.R. Bhasin.
(University of Delhi, 1979).
(Guide : D.S. Aggarwal). 376

Evaluation of English literature course (M.A.) text-book collections of Hindu College, Hansraj College and St. Stephen's College libraries—C. Krishnamoorthy.
(University of Delhi, 1975).
(Guide : M.M. Kashyap). 377

Evaluation of M.A., B.A. and B.Sc. (Hons.) Mathematics textbook collections of Hindu and Hansraj Colleges—K.K. Taneja.
(University of Delhi, 1979).
(Guide : V.K. Sundaram). 378

Evaluation of periodical collections in select medical college libraries in Delhi—Vijayalakshmy.
(University of Delhi, 1982).
(Guide : V.K. Sundaram). 379

Evaluation of textbook collections in History, Political Science, Economics in B.A. (Pass & Hons.) in select colleges—Kasturilal Chugh.
(University of Delhi, 1983).
(Guide : K.N. Gupta). 380

Evaluation of textbook collections in Psychology in the libraries of Delhi College, IP College and Delhi University—Deshraj Singh.
(University of Delhi, 1975).
(Guide : M.M. Kashyap). 381

Evaluation of textbook collections of the libraries of St. Stephen's, Hindu and Kirorimal Colleges in respect of M.A. Economics courses of the University of Delhi—P.N. Pandey.
(University of Delhi, 1975).
(Guide : M.M. Kashyap). 382

Evaluation of the M.A. History textbook collection of Hindu College, Hansraj College and St.

Entry No.

Stephen's College libraries—
Ram Labhaya Sharma.
(University of Delhi, 1975).
(Guide : M.M. Kashyap). 383

Evaluation of the reference sources in the field of Hindi language and literature serving the needs of post-graduates and faculty of Delhi University Campus Colleges—Surinder Mohan Sachdev.
(University of Delhi, 1976).
(Guide : Krishan Kumar). 384

Evaluation of the services : Circulation and Reference in St. Stephen's and K.M. College libraries—Hajra Begum.
(University of Delhi, 1983).
(Guide : K.N. Gupta). 385

Libraries in the evening college of University of Delhi : An examination of their present position and proposals for future development—
J.K. Anand.
(University of Delhi, 1978).
(Guide : Krishan Kumar). 386

Model records for a college library—S. Pandurangam.
(University of Delhi, 1969). 387

Model records of St. Stephen's and K.M. College—
S.S. Sekhon.
(University of Delhi, 1969). 388

Service evaluation of Hindu College library—
Balbir Singh Garg.
(University of Delhi, 1974).
(Guide : M.M. Kashyap). 389

Service evaluation of St. Stephen's College library—
Ram Sarup.
(University of Delhi, 1974).
(Guide : M.M. Kashyap). 390

Staff manual : Draft for college libraries—
Ramesh Kumar.
(University of Delhi, 1975).
(Guide : M.M. Kashyap). 391

Entry No.

Study of the undergraduate libraries of Delhi University Library System—Harish Chandra.
(University of Delhi, 1979).
(Guide : Krishan Kumar). 392

Textbook collections in Political Science for M.A. courses of University of Delhi in Hindu, Daulat Ram and Kirorimal College libraries : A survey—Susheel Kaur.
(University of Delhi, 1976).
(Guide : M.M. Kashyap). 393

Use of recommended books in History and Political Science by B.A. (Hons.) students in I.P. College for Women, Miranda House and Daulat Ram Colleges—Madanlal Popdy.
(University of Delhi, 1984).
(Guide : J.L. Sardana). 394

Academic libraries—College libraries, Gujarat

College libraries under Saurashtra University : A survey—N.H. Barodio.
(Dharwar University, 1980).
(Guide : Kumbhar). 395

Academic libraries—College libraries, Haryana

College libraries in Haryana : A survey—Nate Singh Vatsa.
(Punjab University, 1976). 396

Polytechnic libraries in Haryana : A survey—Wazir Singh Mour.
(Punjab University, 1979). 397

Academic libraries—College libraries, India

Libraries in regional colleges of education in India—Gopal Singh.
(University of Rajasthan, 1979). 398

Academic libraries—College libraries, Karnataka

College libraries in Bijapur city : A survey—

Entry No.

S.B. Patil.
(Dharwar University, 1983).
(Guide : Kumbhar). 399

College libraries in the Karnataka University jurisdiction : A survey—R.C. Patil.
(Dharwar University, 1972).
(Guide : Kumbhar). 400

College libraries under Gulbarga University area : A survey—T.S. Kumar.
(Dharwar University, 1981).
(Guide : Kumbhar). 401

Evaluation of library facilities in colleges affiliated to Bangalore University—M.T. Ramaswamy Gowda.
(University of Mysore, 1974).
(Guide : H.A. Khan). 402

General survey of library resources and services provided in libraries attached to engineering colleges in Karnataka State with special reference to the National Institute of Engineering, Mysore—D.N. Nagarajarao.
(University of Mysore, 1977).
(Guide : P.K. Patil). 403

Growth and development of agricultural education and libraries in India with special reference to Karnataka—K.T. Somashekar.
(University of Mysore, 1973).
(Guide : H.A. Khan). 404

Junior college libraries in Dharwar district : A survey —B.N. Kumbar.
(Dharwar University, 1975).
(Guide : Kumbhar). 405

St. John's Medical College library : A development plan—M.M. Thomas.
(Dharwar University, 1979).
(Guide : Kumbhar). 406

Study of library facilities in colleges of physical education in Karnataka State—S.S. Nagasetty.
(Bangalore University, 1978). 407

Entry No.

Study of library facilities in selected colleges of Mangalore city—D. Venkatesh. (University of Mysore, 1975). (Guide : H.A. Khan). 408

Study of resources of the selected medical college libraries in Karnataka—P.S. Mahesh. (University of Mysore, 1977). (Guide : H.A. Khan). 409

Study of the growth of selected college libraries in Mysore city—M.R. Sannarame Gowda. (University of Mysore, 1977). (Guide : H.A. Khan). 410

Study of the student use of book resources in Regional College of Education library, Mysore—M.J. Subramanya. (University of Mysore, 1975). (Guide : H.A. Khan). 411

Survey of college libraries in Mysore city—Siddappa. (University of Mysore, 1983). (Guide : B. Nagappa). 412

Academic libraries—College libraries, Kerala

Impact of question bank on the reading behaviour of the degree students of Calicut city college —V. Jalaja. (University of Madras, 1979). 413

Libraries in post-graduate colleges in Trivandrum city : A survey with a plan for their development —D. Moni. (Kerala University, 1980). 414

Academic libraries—College libraries, Madhya Pradesh

Organisation and working of libraries in college of education of M. P. : A critical study—B.P. Srivastava. (Vikram University, 1980). (Guide : G.D. Bhargava). 415

Representative general college libraries of Gwalior

Entry No.

city : A survey—S.S. Bhadoria.
(Vikram University, 1981).
(Guide : S.S. Agrawal) 416

Survey of college libraries in Gwalior city—S.S. Singh.
(Vikram University, 1980).
(Guide : S.S. Agrawal). 417

Academic libraries—College libraries, Maharashtra

Growth of college libraries in western Maharashtra —A.C. Tikekar.
(Bombay University, 1970). 418

Libraries in colleges of education affiliated to the University of Bombay—G.D. Sankolli.
(Bombay University, 1975). 419

Use of periodical literature in the medical college libraries of Bombay—M.N. Bhatt.
(SNDT Women's University, 1981). 420

Academic libraries—College libraries, Orissa

Law College library, Cuttack : A study— Padhi Pitambar.
(Dharwar University, 1978).
(Guide : Kumbhar). 421

Libraries of colleges affiliated to the Utkal University—A survey and development plan— B.K. Choudhury.
(Dharwar University, 1979).
(Guide : Kumbhar). 422

Academic libraries—College libraries, Punjab

Problems in the development of library facilities and services in Polytechnics in India, with reference to Punjab—Parmajit Singh Kawatra.
(Punjab University, 1974). 423

Regional Engineering College library, Kurukshetra : A study—Janakraj.
(Punjab University, 1980). 424

Entry No.

Academic libraries—College libraries, Rajasthan

Engineering college libraries in Rajasthan—
N. Sharma.
(University of Rajasthan, 1981). 425

Evaluation of girls college libraries in Jaipur—
Anjali Gargi.
(University of Rajasthan, 1979). 426

Library personnel in college libraries in Jaipur—
Indubala Mathur.
(University of Rajasthan, 1981). 427

Medical college libraries in Rajasthan—
Umesh Agrawal.
(University of Rajasthan, 1978). 428

Survey of Polytechnic libraries in Rajasthan : Field survey—Suresh Chandra Agarwal.
(University of Rajasthan, 1980). 429

Academic libraries—College libraries, Tamil Nadu

Autonomous college libraries in Tamil Nadu : A survey and plan for development—P. Alangarababu.
(Dharwar University, 1980).
(Guide : Kumbhar). 430

College libraries in Madras city : An assessment—
P. Ramalingam.
(University of Madras, 1981). 431

College libraries in Madurai city : A survey—
A.R. Balasubramanian.
(Kamaraj University, 1980).
(Guide : R. Paul Mohan Roy). 432

College libraries in Madurai University area : A survey with a plan for their future development—
S. Gnanamuttu.
(Dharwar University, 1973).
(Guide : Kumbhar). 433

Origin and development of the Madras Law College library : Historical survey—R. Subramanian.
(University of Madras, 1978). 434

Entry No.

Academic libraries—College libraries, Uttar Pradesh

Reading needs in agriculture and the collection of reading materials in agriculture in Central and Agricultural College libraries, BHU—R.R. Deb. (BHU, 1968). 435

Academic libraries—Research libraries

Centre of post-graduate instruction and research library, Panaji (Goa) : A development plan—S.V. Yalagi.
(Dharwar University, 1980).
(Guide : Kumbhar). 436

Evaluation of resources of Central Food Technological Research Institute library, Mysore—M.S. Sreedharappa.
(University of Mysore, 1972).
(Guide : H.A. Khan). 437

Evaluation of selected bibliographical tools available in the library attached to the Indian Institute of Science, Bangalore—M. Chamundeshwari.
(University of Mysore, 1976).
(Guide : P.K. Patil). 438

Growth of IIT libraries, 1972-76—J.N. Pushty.
(BHU, 1979). 439

IIT library and its uses : A field survey—Narinder Kaur.
(University of Rajasthan, 1980). 440

ISRO libraries in India : A study—T.K. Mathew.
(Bombay University, 1980). 441

Kannada Research Institute library : A development plan—S.R. Shetty.
(Dharwar University, 1977).
(Guide : Kumbhar). 442

National Aeronautical Laboratory library : Its resources and services—M. K. Jagadish
(University of Mysore, 1973).
(Guide : H.A. Khan). 443

Post-graduate Centre for Technical Studies library,

Entry No.

Nandihalli : Survey—J.M. Nagaiah.
(Dharwar University, 1983).
(Guide : Kumbhar). 444

Research libraries—M.L. Wali.
(BHU, 1967). 445

Scientific and technical libraries in Chandigarh—Jatinder Kaur.
(Punjab University, 1980). 446

Scientific research and special libraries in India with special reference to Andhra Pradesh—R. Sreepathy Naidu.
(Dharwar University, 1972).
(Guide : Kumbhar). 447

Service evaluation of Delhi School of Social Work library—Vashdev Sharma.
(University of Delhi, 1974).
(Guide : M.M. Kashyap). 448

Study of fluctuation in prices of periodicals subscribed by Rattan Tata Library in the field of Economics and Sociology—V.R. Yadav.
(University of Delhi, 1979).
(Guide : J.L. Sardana). 449

Study of fluctuation in the subscription rates of periodicals subscribed to by Rattan Tata Library during 1978-83—Devraj Singh.
(University of Delhi, 1984).
(Guide : J.L. Sardana). 450

Study of use of periodical literature in Rattan Tata Library—D. Nagajyotsna.
(University of Delhi, 1984).
(Guide : M.M. Kashyap). 451

Survey of Shri Ram Institute for Industrial Research Library—P.K. John.
(University of Delhi, 1977).
(Guide : M.M. Kashyap). 452

Survey of the National Medical Library with regard to its collections, services and use—Lella Dahal.

Entry No.

(University of Delhi, 1977).
(Guide : M.M. Kashyap). 453

Academic libraries—School libraries

Multipurpose demonstration school library : A case study—Lalithamba.
(University of Mysore, 1981).
(Guide : B. Nagappa). 454

School library—Parasnath.
(BHU, 1967). 455

Academic libraries—School libraries, Andhra Pradesh

High school libraries in Chittoor district (AP) : A survey—P. Kamaih.
(Dharwar University, 1978).
(Guide : Kumbhar). 456

Report of a survey of secondary school libraries in Visakhapatnam—K. Ranirao.
(Andhra University, 1980).
(Guide : K. Sivareddy). 457

Academic libraries—School libraries, Chandigarh

Government model high school libraries in Chandigarh : A survey—Ashu Bhalla.
(Punjab University, 1983). 458

Organisation and administration of public school libraries in Chandigarh—Satindu Kaur.
(Punjab University, 1982). 459

Academic libraries—School libraries, Delhi

Evaluation of textbook collection at undergraduate level in economics, political science and history in the library of school of correspondence courses—Reeta Dua.
(University of Delhi, 1984).
(Guide : D.S. Aggarwal). 460

Problems of book selection, acquisition and building in the higher secondary school libraries in Delhi—

Entry No.

Virendra Jain.
(University of Delhi, 1971).
(Guide : B.V.R. Rao). 461

Survey of secondary school libraries in the Union Territory of Delhi : A field report—Yash Pal Chhabra.
(University of Delhi, 1976).
(Guide : Krishan Kumar). 462

Academic libraries—School libraries, Karnataka

School libraries in Udupi : A survey—U.R. Maiya.
(Dharwar University, 1982).
(Guide : Kumbhar). 463

Secondary school libraries in Dharwar Corporation area : A survey—S.V. Jamadar.
(Dharwar University, 1974).
(Guide : Kumbhar). 464

Secondary school libraries in Gulbarga city : A survey—S.R. Mullur.
(Dharwar University, 1983).
(Guide : Kumbhar). 465

Study of the library facilities in some selected schools at Bangalore and Mysore—C.K. Pattanashetti.
(University of Mysore, 1976).
(Guide : T.V. Subramanyam). 466

Survey of school libraries in Mysore city—Somashekar.
(University of Mysore, 1983).
(Guide : B. Nagappa). 467

Academic libraries—School libraries, Madhya Pradesh

Higher secondary school libraries of Indore city and their services : A survey—Naliniranjan Purohit.
(Vikram University, 1978).
(Guide : A. Tejomurty). 468

Academic libraries—School libraries, Maharashtra

Investigation into the organisation and use of secon-

Entry No.

dary school libraries in Bombay city—V.P. Save. (Bombay University, 1974). 469

Library facilities in central schools of Pune and Bombay area : A survey—A.G. Sherikar. (Dharwar University, 1981). (Guide : Kumbhar). 470

Resources and services of secondary school libraries in Pune—M.B. Konnur. (Poona University, 1980). (Guide : D.W. Shewde). 471

School libraries with particular reference to Kolhapur district—R.G. Salvi. (Dharwar University, 1972). (Guide : Kumbhar). 472

Academic libraries—School libraries, Tamil Nadu

High school libraries in Madurai city : A survey—S.D. Jacob. (Dharwar University, 1977). (Guide : Kumbhar). 473

Higher secondary school libraries in Tirunelveli district : A survey—D. Solomon. (Kamaraj University, 1980). (Guide : D.B. Krishnarao) 474

Library facilities in higher secondary schools in Madras : A survey—P. Rajagopalan. (University of Madras, 1981). 475

Academic libraries—University libraries

Divisional libraries in universities—P. Purnachandrarao. (Andhra University, 1980). (Guide : B. Vijayalakshmi). 476

University libraries in developing countries—Indra Bumb. (University of Rajasthan, 1977). 477

Academic libraries—University libraries, Administration

Changing dimension of university library administra-

Entry No.

tion—Rajan Kumar.
(University of Rajasthan, 1979). 478

Financial administration in university libraries : A literature survey—Alka Bharadwaj.
(University of Rajasthan, 1979). 479

Model staff manual for a university library—A.G. Ghan.
(Punjab University, 1971). 480

Motivational dynamics and work efficiency in the university libraries—Jugal Kishor Khanna.
(Punjab University, 1980). 481

Recent trends in the administration and organisation in university libraries—Kawaljit Singh.
(Punjab University, 1979). 482

Staff management in university libraries—Pushpalata Agarwal.
(University of Rajasthan, 1981). 483

Technical services in university libraries : Literature survey—Arvinder Kaur.
(University of Rajasthan, 1980). 484

Academic libraries—University libraries, Andhra Pradesh

Nagarjuna University library : A development plan—J. Ramarao.
(Dharwar University, 1977).
(Guide : Kumbhar). 485

Origin, growth and development of Sri Venkateswara University library—K. Nagaraja Naidu.
(Bangalore University, 1979). 486

Srikrishnadevaraya University library : A development plan—D.C. Ankireddy.
(Dharwar University, 1983).
(Guide : Kumbhar). 487

Sri Venkateswara University library—J. Muralidhar.
(Andhra University, 1980).
(Guide : K. Sarada). 488

Use of periodicals : A case study of the Department of Chemistry, Andhra University—

Entry No.

S.S. Janardanarao.
(Andhra University, 1980).
(Guide : G.V.S.L.N. Raju). 489

Academic libraries—University libraries, Assam

North-Eastern Hill University library : A survey in retrospect—M. Satyanarayana.
(Andhra University, 1981).
(Guide : K. Sivareddy). 490

Staff and services in Assam Agricultural University library : A comparative study with ICAR norms—M. Islam.
(BHU, 1978). 491

Academic libraries—University libraries, Collection

Bangalore University library : its origin and development—P. Sadashivamurthy.
(University of Mysore, 1977). 492
(Guide : P.K. Patil).

Basic literature in the field of Botany in Punjab University library, Chandigarh : A survey—Sarojini Mehta.
(Punjab University, 1975). 493

Basic literature in the field of Economics in Punjab University library, Chandigarh : A survey—Anju Baweja.
(Punjab University, 1976). 494

Basic literature in the field of Fine Arts in Punjab University library, Chandigarh : A survey—Anita Jain.
(Punjab University, 1976). 495

Basic literature in the field of Indian History in Punjab University library, Chandigarh : A survey—Kulwant Singh.
(Punjab University, 1975). 496

Basic literature in the field of Physics in Punjab University library, Chandigarh : A survey—Mohinder Singh Chauhan.
(Punjab University, 1975). 497

Entry No.

Basic literature in the field of Political Science in Punjab University library, Chandigarh : A survey —Shashibala Anand.
(Punjab University, 1976). 498

Basic literature in the field of Sociology in Punjab University library, Chandigarh : A survey— Sewa Singh.
(Punjab University, 1976). 499

Evaluation of English literature collection in the University of Poona library—Sivani Sengupta.
(Poona University, 1981). 500
(Guide : M.R. Riswadkar).

Evaluation of library resources of Himachal Pradesh University, Palampur campus in the field of Agriculture—C.D. Handa.
(Punjab University, 1973). 501

Evaluation of library resources of Punjab University library in the field of Mathematics—V.P. Bhalla.
(Punjab University, 1973). 502

Evaluation of library resources of Punjab University library and Law department library in the field of Indian Law—Kirpal Singh.
(Punjab University, 1973). 503

Evaluation of periodicals collection in selected university libraries in Delhi—V. Subramanian.
(University of Delhi, 1982).
(Guide : V.K. Sundaram). 504

Evaluation of resources of Commonwealth literature in the Mysore University library—A.C. Kalamma.
(University of Mysore, 1980).
(Guide : P.K. Patil). 505

Evaluation of textbook collection for M.A. Sociology courses in Rattan Tata Library and JNU library— Hansraj Hajatri.
(University of Delhi, 1975).
(Guide : M.M. Kashyap). 506

Evaluation of the library resources in the field of

Entry No.

English literature in the University of Mysore—T.V. Subramanyam. (University of Mysore, 1972). (Guide : P.K. Patil). 507

Identification and collection of materials relating to the recent economic, social and political changes in Kerala in the Kerala University—A.V. Rahelamma. (University of Mysore, 1980). (Guide : H.A. Khan). 508

Identification of the core literature in information science for the Master of Library and Information Science programme and an evaluation of the Kerala University library book collection in the area—Pushpa Raghavaiah. (Kerala University, 1980). 509

Literature on physical education in Punjab University : A survey—Indu Kalia. (Punjab University, 1979). 510

Study of curricular and co-curricular book collection of Department of Education of University of Delhi—Mahendra Pal. (University of Delhi, 1982). (Guide : K.N. Gupta). 511

Study of resources of Delhi University library system in Anthropology—Shashi Gupta. (University of Delhi, 1977). (Guide : K.N. Gupta). 512

Study of resources of Delhi University library system in Botany—Jagdish Arora. (University of Delhi, 1977). (Guide : J.L. Sardana). 513

Study of resources of Delhi University library system in Hindi language and literature—Madhubala Sharma. (University of Delhi, 1977). (Guide : D.S. Aggarwal). 514

Study of resources of Delhi University library system

Entry No.

in Mathematics—Sushil Kumar Sharma.
(University of Delhi, 1977).
(Guide : C.P. Vashisth). 515

Study of resources of Delhi University library system in Physics—Renu Arora.
(University of Delhi, 1977).
(Guide : C.P. Vashisth). 516

Study of resources of Delhi University library system in Sociology—Satya Pal.
(University of Delhi, 1977).
(Guide : D.S. Aggarwal). 517

Study of resources of Delhi University library system in Statistics—Sudha Aggarwal.
(University of Delhi, 1977).
(Guide : K.N. Gupta). 518

Study of resources of Delhi University library system in Zoology—Ravinder Kumar Chandra.
(University of Delhi, 1977).
(Guide : D.S. Aggarwal). 519

Study of resources of DUL system, JNU library and Sapru House library in Political Science—Rekha Jain.
(University of Delhi, 1977).
(Guide : M.M. Kashyap). 520

Study of the resources of the Mysore University library in the field of Botany—B.S. Maheswarappa.
(University of Mysore, 1980).
(Guide : B. Nagappa). 521

Study of the resources of the Mysore University library in the field of Economics—K. Leela.
(University of Mysore, 1976).
(Guide : H.A. Khan). 522

Study of the resources of the Mysore University library in the field of Psychology—S.G. Jayashree.
(University of Mysore, 1975).
(Guide : H.A. Khan). 523

Study of the resources of the Mysore University library

Entry No.

in the field of Sociology—K.N. Raju.
(University of Mysore, 1976).
(Guide : H.A. Khan). 524

Survey of biographical resources in the Mysore University library—K.S. Gopinath.
(University of Mysore, 1976).
(Guide : T.V. Subramanyam). 525

Survey of literature in History in the Punjab University library, Chandigarh—Brij Mohini Sud.
(Punjab University, 1978). 526

Survey of literature in Philosophy in the Punjab University library, Chandigarh—Neeta Khanna.
(Punjab University, 1978). 527

Survey of Zoology literature in the Punjab University library, Chandigarh—Navjeet Kaur.
(Punjab University, 1978). 528

Academic libraries—University libraries, Delhi

Acquisition of books and financial management in DUL system—Prem Singh.
(University of Delhi, 1983).
(Guide : D.S. Aggarwal). 529

Acquisition section of the University of Delhi library—S.D. Vyas.
(University of Delhi, 1971).
(Guide : B.V.R. Rao). 530

Analysis of the current serial publications being subscribed to in Delhi University library system, JNU and IIT library—Manjula Bhatnagar.
(University of Delhi, 1977).
(Guide : M.M. Kashyap). 531

Comparative study of centralisation versus decentralisation in JNU library and Delhi University library—A.K. Verma.
(University of Delhi, 1980).
(Guide : V.K. Sundaram). 532

Compare and suggest ways of minimising the cost of processing of reading materials in the JNU library

Entry No.

and IIT, Delhi library—Rajkumari.
(University of Delhi, 1978).
(Guide : J.L. Sardana). 533

Delhi University library system, 1965-74—
Asha Chitkara.
(University of Rajasthan, 1979). 534

Draft procedural manual for the acquisition section of Delhi University library—Trilok Chand.
(University of Delhi, 1970).
(Guide : M.M. Kashyap). 535

Academic libraries—University libraries, Delhi

Draft procedural manual for the circulation section of the University of Delhi library—M. Bavakutty.
(University of Delhi, 1970).
(Guide : M.M. Kashyap). 536

Draft procedural manual for the periodical section of the University of Delhi library—V.S. Rastogi.
(University of Delhi, 1970).
(Guide : M.M. Kashyap). 537

Evaluation of library collection of South Campus library—Suman Bhatiani.
(University of Delhi, 1983).
(Guide : C.P. Vashisth). 538

Evaluation of reference service in JNU library—S. Majumdar.
(University of Delhi, 1980).
(Guide : C.P. Vashisth). 539

Evaluation of the services provided by the circulation and reference section of Delhi University central library—Ashok Kumar.
(University of Delhi, 1978).
(Guide : D.S. Aggarwal). 540

Evaluation of the services provided by the circulation and reference departments of JNU library—Sarman Lal.
(University of Delhi, 1978).
(Guide : M.M. Kashyap). 541

Entry No.

Financial administration of the University of Delhi library—Neena Sud.
(University of Delhi, 1971).
(Guide : B.V.R. Rao) 542

Personnel management in DULS and JNU library—Sunil Dutt.
(University of Delhi, 1983).
(Guide : D.S. Aggarwal). 543

Price fluctuation in History and Political Science periodicals subscribed in Delhi University library—Manju Zutshi.
(University of Delhi, 1979).
(Guide : V.K. Sundaram). 544

Readers services of University of Delhi library—Baljeet.
(University of Delhi, 1971).
(Guide : B.V.R. Rao). 545

Study of the use of periodical literature in Delhi University library—Kodandaramaiah.
(University of Delhi, 1984).
(Guide : M.M. Kashyap). 546

Trends in administrative organisation of university libraries with particular reference to JNU library system—G.A. Sastri.
(University of Delhi, 1981).
(Guide : P.B. Mangla). 547

Use of periodical literature in Jamia Milia Islamia library—Shakila Begum.
(University of Delhi, 1984).
(Guide : D.S. Aggarwal). 548

Academic libraries—University libraries, India

Development of academic libraries with special reference to university libraries in India—A.L. Wadikar.
(Vikram University, 1974).
(Guide : G.D. Bhargava). 549

Development of university libraries in India—

Entry No.

B.B. Hungund.
(Bombay University, 1969). 550

Development of university libraries in India in post-independence period : A study—Mohanlal.
(Punjab University, 1976). 551

Inter-library loan services in university libraries in India : A study—Jugal Kishore.
(Punjab University, 1972). 552

Library personnel in university libraries in India : A study—Vinod Kumar Grover.
(Punjab University, 1978). 553

University libraries in India—Manorama Kothari.
(Punjab University, 1978). 554

Academic libraries—University libraries, Karnataka

Bibliometric study of the Ph.D. theses submitted to the University of Mysore in the field of History—Narinder Kaur Bains.
(University of Mysore, 1983).
(Guide : Khaiser Jahan Begum). 555

Cost analysis in Mysore University library—N. Bhaskar Reddy.
(University of Mysore, 1978).
(Guide : N.B. Pangannaya). 556

Gulbarga University library : A development plan—M.V. Danappanavar.
(Dharwar University, 1981).
(Guide : Kumbhar). 557

Karnataka University library : A development plan—T.L. Byadgi.
(Dharwar University, 1973).
(Guide : Kumbhar). 558

Mysore University library catalogue use study—H.J. Poornachandrarao.
(University of Mysore, 1981).
(Guide : N.B. Pangannaya). 559

Mysore University library : Its origin and development—B. Nagappa.

Entry No.

(University of Mysore, 1972).
(Guide : P.K. Patil). 560

Services in the university libraries of Karnataka : A study—J.P. Hiremath.
(Dharwar University, 1981).
(Guide : Kumbhar). 561

Study of serials control in Mysore University library—M. Manjunatha.
(University of Mysore, 1982).
(Guide : B. Nagappa). 562

University library, Dharwar : A study and development plan—V.R. Kotre.
(Dharwar University, 1983).
(Guide : Kumbhar). 563

Use of social science periodicals in Mysore University library—Khaiser Jahan Begum.
(University of Mysore, 1979).
(Guide : H.A. Khan). 564

Utilization of UGC book grants (1976-79) : A case study of Mysore University library, 1981—Ponnamma Devaiah.
(University of Mysore, 1981).
(Guide : H.A. Khan). 565

Academic libraries—University libraries, Kerala

Acquisition policies and procedures in university libraries in Kerala with special reference to Kerala University library, 1975-80—S. Issac Shakuntala.
(Kerala University, 1980). 566

Catalogue and its use : A detailed study of the use made of the main catalogue in the Kerala University library by the users—P. Suvarnakumari.
(Kerala University, 1981). 567

Centralization and decentralization university libraries in the States of Kerala and Karnataka—C.V. Usharani.
(SNDT Women's University, 1981). 568

Entry No.

Resource allocation decisions in university library and information services for developing countries with reference to the Calicut University—
Raju M. Mathew.
(University of Madras, 1979). 569

Study of the order supply correlations of books in the Kerala University library, Calicut University library and Cochin University library—
K.P. Somanathan Nair.
(Kerala University, 1982). 570

Use pattern of periodical literature in biological sciences : A study conducted in the libraries of the Departments of Botany, Zoology and Acquatic Biology and Fisheries of the University of Kerala—
P.K. Mohanan.
(Kerala University, 1981). 571

Academic libraries—University libraries, Maharashtra

SNDT Women's University library and its branches : A study—M.R. Gandhi.
(SNDT Women's University, 1981). 572

Academic libraries—University libraries, Orissa

Literature use by the faculty members of the Utkal University—P. Subudhi.
(BHU, 1979). 573

University libraries in Orissa : A field survey—
Prahallad Panda.
(University of Rajasthan, 1979). 574

Utkal University library : A study—R.K. Rout.
(Dharwar University, 1976).
(Guide : Kumbhar). 575

Academic libraries—University libraries, Punjab

Acquisition of periodicals : A case study of Punjab University library, PGI library and SCI—
Harpreet Walia.
(Punjab University, 1977). 576

Entry No.

Documentation in university libraries with special reference to Punjab Agricultural University library, Punjab University library—Baljit Arneja.
(Punjab University, 1977). 577

Planning of library cum workshop for the Department of Library Science, Punjab University, Chandigarh—Geeta.
(Punjab University, 1981). 578

Punjab University library : A case study—H.S. Bajwa.
(University of Rajasthan, 1979). 579

Rare books available on Fine Arts in Punjab University library : A study—Rekha Malhotra.
(Punjab University, 1977). 580

Study of special collections, their collectors, donations and organisation in the Punjab university library—Iqbal Singh.
(Punjab University, 1982). 581

Academic libraries—University libraries, Rajasthan.

Departmental libraries in Rajasthan University and their uses : Field survey—Alka Bhargava.
(University of Rajasthan, 1980). 582

Jodhpur University library : A survey of services based on users opinion—D.C. Ojha.
(BHU, 1976). 583

Rajasthan University library : A field survey—A.K. Gautum.
(University of Rajasthan, 1979). 584

Subject cataloguing in the university libraries of Rajasthan—R.K. Dave.
(BHU, 1976). 585

University of Udaipur library system : A survey—Laxmi Narayan Verma.
(University of Rajasthan, 1981). 586

University libraries in Rajasthan : A field survey—M.C. Saxena.
(University of Rajasthan. 1979). 587

Entry No.

Academic libraries—University libraries, Tamil Nadu.

Annamalai University library—T. Padmanabhan.
(University of Madras, 1981). 588

Assessment of the development of Madurai University library—D. Chandran.
(University of Mysore, 1974).
(Guide : B. Nagappa). 589

Gandhigram Rural University library : A development plan—N. Arumugam.
(Kamaraj University, 1982).
(Guide : D. Chandran). 590

Study centres in Madurai-Kamaraj University area : A survey—Cyril Royappa.
(Kamaraj University, 1980).
(Guide : D. Chandran). 591

Academic libraries—University libraries, Uttar Pradesh.

Technical, processing of books in G.B. Pant University of Agriculture and Technology : A work study—R.P. Singh.
(BHU, 1978). 592

Technical workflow in the university libraries of Varanasi--G.C. Srivastava.
(BHU, 1968). 593

Treatment of government publications in university libraries of Varanasi—A.R. Singh.
(BHU, 1968). 594

Use of library catalogue of the BHU central library—G.P. Singh.
(BHU, 1978). 595

Associations

Andhra Pradesh Library Association : A study—K. Sarada.
(University of Mysore, 1974).
(Guide : H.A. Khan). 596

Andhra Pradesh Library Association : Origin and development, activities and achievements—

Entry No.

A. Jayadev.
(Punjab University, 1983). 597

Classification Research Group : Its genesis, growth and contribution to library classification research—Ravikant Pahuja.
(Punjab University, 1983). 598

Contribution of the Kerala Granthasala Sangham in the development of libraries in Kerala—N. Muralidharan Nair.
(Kerala University, 1980). 599

Contribution of Unesco towards the betterment of library facilities throughout the world—S.C. Aggarwal.
(Punjab University, 1973). 600

Delhi Library Association : Its role, achievements and future—Shakuntala Rani.
(University of Delhi, 1976).
(Guide : M.M. Kashyap). 601

FID, 80 years elapsed : A critical study—Shaista Wahab Maiwandi.
(University of Delhi, 1976).
(Guide : M.M. Kashyap). 602

IFLA : A study of its origin, development, activities and achievements—Santosh Kumari.
(Punjab University, 1983). 603

Indian Library Association and its role in the development of library profession in India—Kuldeep Rani Bharadwaj.
(University of Delhi, 1976).
(Guide : Krishan Kumar). 604

Library associations—Ram Swaroop Sharma.
(BHU, 1967). 605

Library associations in India : USA and UK—S. Hada.
(University of Rajasthan, 1978). 606

Presidents of ILA, 1933-82 : A survey of their writings—Ajai Pal Kaur.
(Punjab University, 1984). 607

Entry No.

Role of library associations towards the advancement of library profession with reference to UK, USA and India—Barjindev Pal.
(Punjab University, 1981). 608

Role of Unesco in library development, 1946-75—Ramesh Chander Chibber.
(University of Delhi, 1976).
(Guide : Krishan Kumar). 609

Role of Unesco in the development of bibliography and documentation—Jaspal Kaur.
(Punjab University, 1981). 610

Role of Unesco in the development of libraries, archives and information services in India—Omar Moalim Muse.
(University of Delhi, 1983).
(Guide : P.B. Mangla). 611

Role of Unesco in the development of library and information services in Africa—D.G. Sangal.
(BHU, 1976). 612

Role of Unesco in the development of public libraries in Africa, Asia and Latin America—Kamlesh Kumari Bansal.
(Punjab University, 1984). 613

United Nations Depository centres in India : A survey—S.B. Kittur.
(Dharwar University, 1979).
(Guide : Kumbhar). 614

Unesco's role in the development of libraries and archives in Asian countries—H.K. Jha.
(BHU, 1975). 615

Automation

Application of computers to libraries : A literature survey—Veena Rampal.
(Punjab University, 1974). 616

Automation and data processing in libraries—Indra Kaul.
(University of Rajasthan, 1979). 617

Entry No.

Automation in libraries—P. Dhyani.
(BHU, 1971). 618
Automation in libraries—Dalbir Singh.
(University of Rajasthan, 1978). 619
Computer applications in Indian libraries—P.M. Keeka.
(SNDT Women's University, 1981). 620
Computer for library and information work and its status in India—Satnam Singh Pal.
(Punjab University, 1983). 621
Computerization of routines for the acquisition of serials : An experiment with IBM 1620 computer—P.K. Sinha.
(INSDOC, 1969).
(Guide : A.S. Raizada). 622
Contribution of Japan for automation in libraries—Neelam Sood.
(Punjab University, 1977). 623
Place of library automation in education for librarianship in India : A study—Rashmi Batra.
(Punjab University, 1983). 624
Use of Elliot 803 B for stock verification in libraries—S. Nigam.
(INSDOC, 1971).
(Guide : A.S. Raizada). 625

Business libraries

Business libraries—R.M. Khan.
(BHU, 1966). 626

Business libraries—Commerce

Commercial lending libraries in the metropolitan city of Madras—P. Perumal.
(University of Madras, 1978). 627

Business libraries—Economics

Evaluation of acquisition policy and proceedings of periodicals in the Indian Institute of Foreign

Entry No.

Trade Library and Rattan Tata library—Pankaj Sircar.
(University of Delhi, 1979).
(Guide : M.M. Kashyap). 628

Business libraries—Engineering

Engineering libraries in Punjab : A survey—P.S. Kang.
(Punjab University, 1979). 629

Business libraries—Films

Management of film libraries with special reference to Bombay-Pune region—Aparna S. Phadke.
(Poona University, 1980).
(Guide : M.R. Riswadkar). 630

Organisation of film libraries : A survey of film libraries in Delhi—G. Radhakrishna.
(INSDOC, 1967).
(Guide : T.N. Rajan). 631

Business libraries—Fine Arts

Libraries of Sahitya Akademy, Sangeet Natak Akademy and Lalit Kala Akademy : A comparative study of their services and uses—C.S. Shanta.
(University of Delhi, 1984).
(Guide : C.P. Vashisth). 632

Organisation and administration of a Fine Art library—Vinod Kanwar.
(Punjab University, 1983). 633

Business libraries—Government

Evaluation of reference collection in Central Secretariat Library—Amita Mehrotra.
(University of Delhi, 1983).
(Guide : J.L. Sardana). 634

Government departmental libraries in Jaipur—Dinesh Kumar Natani.
(University of Rajasthan, 1981). 635

Entry No.

Survey of government documents in Central Secretariat Library—Meena Arora.
(University of Delhi, 1980). 636

Business libraries—Industry

Industrial libraries in Gujarat—Y.A. Mehta.
(Bombay University, 1976). 637

Role of industrial libraries in Maharashtra—L.M. Patil.
(Bombay University, 1972). 638

Business libraries—Manuscripts

Manuscript libraries : A study of organisation, care and use of manuscripts in the libraries of Varanasi—Ramjee Singh.
(BHU, 1979). 639

Manuscript libraries : Their administration and organisation—Ranjit Kaur.
(Punjab University, 1983). 640

Business libraries—Medicine

Evaluation of periodical collection in select medical libraries in Delhi—Vijayalakshmi Subramanian.
(University of Delhi, 1982).
(Guide : V.K. Sundaram). 641

Medical libraries in India after 1947 and their future—Pradeep Kumar.
(Punjab University, 1977). 642

Medical libraries in Kerala—N. Gopinathan Nair.
(Dharwar University, 1980).
(Guide : Kumbhar). 643

Medical library—Lakshminarain.
(BHU, 1970). 644

Study of the availability of medical periodicals in Delhi medical libraries—S.K. Chadha.
(INSDOC, 1974).
(Guide : B. Guha). 645

Entry No.

Business libraries—Newspapers

Newspapers libraries in Bombay and Pune—
S.R. Bulakh.
(Bombay University, 1975). 646

Business libraries—Pharmaceuticals

Pharmaceutical industrial libraries in Bombay—
P.R. Dadarkar.
(SNDT Women's University, 1983). 647

Planning a library for medium size pharmaceutical industry—Umarani Gupta.
(Punjab University, 1981). 648

Business libraries—Railways

Survey of railways libraries in India—B.K. Singh.
(BHU, 1972). 649

Business libraries—Science

Bibliographical services in scientific and technical libraries in Delhi : A survey—Ashok Kumar.
(University of Delhi, 1984).
(Guide : Krishan Kumar). 650

Business libraries—Technical

Evaluation and comparative study of IIT library and IARI library with regard to administrative organisation, staffing pattern and services—B.S. Nigam.
(University of Delhi, 1980).
(Guide : P.B. Mangla). 651

Examination of the organization, procedures and services of the photoduplication department of IIT, Delhi library—
V.K. Sankaran Namboodripad.
(University of Delhi, 1978).
(Guide : M.M. Kashyap). 652

Organisation of a technical library in BHEL, Tiruchirapalli—V. Subramanian.
(INSDOC, 1965).
(Guide : T.S. Rajagopalan). 653

Entry No.

Scientific and technical libraries in Bhopal city : A survey—B.N. Arora. (Vikram University, 1980). (Guide : A. Tejomurty). 654

Technical college libraries in Rewa district (MP) : A survey—Sunil Kamal Misra. (Vikram University, 1981). (Guide : A. Tejomurty). 655

Cataloguing

Catalogue and cataloguing methods adopted in the libraries of the constituent and affiliated colleges of the University of Poona—D.W. Shewde. (Bombay University, 1971). 656

Catalogue card reproduction at local level—S.C. Verma. (University of Delhi, 1970). 657

Catalogue card reproduction at national level—Niraj Kant Duggal. (University of Delhi, 1969). 658

Cataloguing operation in major libraries of 'Twin Cities' of Hyderabad and Secunderabad : A survey—Yadagiri Reddy. (Osmania University, 1980). 659

On-Line cataloguing : A state of art survey—Anita Mahajan. (Punjab University, 1983). 660

Cataloguing—AACR

AACR : A comparative study of first and second editions—Vandana Aggarwal. (Punjab University, 1981). 661

Comparative study of AACR-I and AACR-II—A.N. Geetha. (University of Mysore, 1981). (Guide : Khaiser Jahan Begum). 662

Entry No.

Comparative study of rules for descriptive cataloguing of books, pamphlets and printed sheets in AACR-I and AACR-II—Madhu Goel.
(University of Delhi, 1982).
(Guide : K.N. Gupta). 663

History and Development of Anglo-American Code : A study—A. Kamakshi.
(Dharwar University, 1977).
(Guide : Kumbhar). 664

Cataloguing—AACR and CCC

AACR and CCC : A comparative study—P.C. Mathur.
(Punjab University, 1977). 665

Corporate author : A critical study of the rules of AACR and CCC—V.S.L. Srivastava.
(BHU, 1976). 666

Critical study of the treatment of conflict of authorship according to CCC (Ed 5), AACR (North American Text) (Ed 1) and AACR (Ed 2)—G. Sobhana.
(Kerala University, 1982). 667

Ranganathan's CCC and AACR—Matwal Chand.
(Punjab University, 1974). 668

Cataloguing—Author and Title

Author and title cataloguing, 1961-71—S.S. Agrawal.
(BHU, 1972). 669

Cataloguing—Canons

Canon of recall value and readers' approach to documents—Singh.
(BHU, 1978). 670

Cataloguing—Contribution

Contribution of Ranganathan in the field of cataloguing—Satwant Singh.
(Punjab University, 1971). 671

Entry No.

Contribution to cataloguing by Panizzi and Cutter—M.K. Bhandi.
(Dharwar University, 1976).
(Guide : Kumbhar). 672

Development in the field of library cataloguing since 1950 with special reference to the contributions of IFLA, ALA and Library Association, London—Inderjeet.
(University of Delhi, 1977).
(Guide : K.N. Gupta). 673

Cataloguing—Cooperative and Centralized

Centralized and cooperative cataloguing—P.C. Jain.
(University of Rajasthan, 1975). 674

Origin and development of cooperative and centralized cataloguing in USA—Jagtar Singh.
(Punjab University, 1980). 675

Cataloguiug—Corporate authorship

Analytical study of the provisions relating to corporate bodies in cataloguing codes—R. Shalini.
(University of Mysore, 1975).
(Guide : K.S. Raghavan). 676

Concept of corporate authorship—O.P. Grover.
(University of Rajasthan, 1979). 677

Development and problems of corporate authors in cataloguing with special reference to Indian official publications—Sayed Ahmed Karim.
(University of Delhi, 1964). 678

Treatment of personal and corporate authorship in the different editions of the CCC—A Ramasamy.
(Kamaraj University, 1981).
(Guide : D. Chandran). 679

Cataloguing—History

Development and trends in cataloguing in twentieth century—Y.P. Dubey.
(BHU, 1979). 680

Entry No.

Historical development of catalogue codes : Literature survey—Mahendar Grodara.
(University of Rajasthan, 1980). 681

Recent developments in cataloguing, 1967-77—T. Das.
(University of Rajasthan, 1978). 682

Cataloguing—Indic names

Indic names—R.K. Kaul.
(BHU, 1972). 683

Problems in rendering of Indic names—Shantilal Dave.
(Punjab University, 1977). 684

Structure and rendering of Indian Muslim names—Mohd. Haroon.
(University of Delhi, 1982).
(Guide : K.N. Gupta). 685

Cataloguing—Rules

Cataloguing rules—K.G. Tyagi.
(BHU, 1967). 686

Proposed cataloguing rules for maps and coins according to CCC—S. Subbalakshmi.
(University of Delhi, 1975).
(Guide : M.M. Kashyap). 687

Proposed cataloguing rules for sound recordings in CCC—Aruna Arora.
(University of Delhi, 1975).
(Guide : M.M. Kashyap). 688

Proposed draft rules for cataloguing films, microfilms and photocopies according to CCC—R.A. Ramasastry.
(University of Delhi, 1975).
(Guide : M.M. Kashyap). 689

Cataloguing—Subject headings

Analysis of terminology, form and structure of subject headings in Punjabi literature and formulation of rules for headings in Punjabi language—

Entry No.

S. Trikha.
(Punjab University, 1972). 690

Efficiency of subject headings in Kannada : Formulated on the basis of postulate of Absolute Syntax—G. Chandramma.
(Bangalore University, 1977). 691

Subject headings—G.S. Singh.
(BHU, 1968). 692

Subject headings : A critical study—Devraj Sharma.
(Vikram University, 1982).
(Guide : S.S. Agrawal). 693

Citation analysis

A vs. B : A journal citation study in a special discipline—Jairam Kaushik.
(Punjab University, 1984). 694

Characteristics of botanical literature : Citation study of doctoral dissertations : An enquiry into the adequacy of periodical literature in Mysore University library—B.P. Prakash.
(University of Mysore, 1982).
(Guide : B.S. Maheswarappa). 695

Characteristics of Indian agricultural information sources : A citation analysis of Indian Journal of Agricultural Sciences—Jagdish Chand Jain.
(Punjab University, 1983). 696

Citation analysis and use of scientific periodicals by dairy scientists in India—N.C. Sharma.
(BHU, 1977). 697

Citation analysis as a tool in journal evaluation : A study of Indian scientific journals—Arvind K. Shrivastava.
(Vikram University, 1981).
(Guide : S.S. Agrawal) 698

Citation analysis of theses in Anthropology submitted to Delhi University—Gurmeet Kaur.
(University of Delhi, 1983).
(Guide : M.M. Kashyap). 699

Entry No.

Citation analysis of theses in Chemistry submitted to Delhi University—Manojkumar Misra.
(University of Delhi, 1982).
(Guide : M.M. Kashyap). 700

Citation analysis of theses in Economics submitted to Delhi University—Madan Lal.
(University of Delhi, 1982).
(Guide : J.L. Sardana). 701

Citation analysis of theses in Physics submitted to Delhi University—Surender Kumar.
(University of Delhi, 1982).
(Guide : Krishan Kumar). 702

Citation analysis of theses in Physics submitted to Delhi University—S.K. Tyagi.
(University of Delhi, 1982).
(Guide : M.M. Kashyap). 703

Citation analysis of theses in Political Science submitted to Delhi University—Devinder Kaur.
(University of Delhi, 1983).
(Guide : P.B. Mangla). 704

Citation analysis of theses in Social Sciences presented by research scholars to Jiwaji University, Gwalior during 1975-80—Manojbala Khare.
(Vikram University, 1981).
(Guide : G.D. Bhargava). 705

Citation analysis studies of periodicals in Zoology—U.N. Mathur.
(University of Delhi, 1984).
(Guide : M.M. Kashyap). 706

Citation behaviour of American and Indian agricultural economists : A case study—K.V. Rajarao.
(Andhra University, 1981).
(Guide : K. Sivareddy). 707

Citation behaviour of Indian biologists : A case study—V. Balaramireddy.
(Andhra University, 1981).
(Guide : B. Vijayalakshmi). 708

Entry No.

Citation behaviour of Indian chemists : A case study—P. Ratnakumar.
(Andhra University, 1980).
(Guide : B. Vijayalakshmi). 709

Citation characteristics of agronomy literature in doctoral theses of BHU—M.L. Kulkarni.
(BHU, 1976). 710

Citation patterns in the literature of Library Science : An analytical study—S.S. Santaram.
(Dharwar University, 1979).
(Guide : Kumbhar). 711

Leisure : A citation study—S. Kumaraswamy.
(University of Mysore, 1981).
(Guide : N.B. Pangannaya). 712

Pilot study on bibliometric analysis of citations in select 29 Ph.D. theses in Physics awarded by the Madurai-Kamaraj University during the period 1970-80—M. Raghuram.
(Kamaraj University, 1982).
(Guide : D.B. Krishnarao). 713

Pilot study on some aspects of citation analysis of select doctoral theses from the department of Biological Sciences—Ushadevi Jeyraj.
(Kamaraj University, 1981).
(Guide : D.B. Krishnarao). 714

Psychology : A citation analysis study—V. Rama Choudary.
(University of Madras, 1981). 715

Report on the literature citations in the field of engineering and technology as seen in Indian engineering periodicals during 1955-59—K. Hariharaprasad.
(INSDOC, 1965).
(Guide : B. Guha). 716

Report on the study of the literature citations in the field of Botany as seen in Indian botanical periodicals during the period 1955-59 : A statistical analysis—T. Viswanadham.

Entry No.

(INSDOC, 1965).
(Guide : B. Guha). 717

Study of the citation practice of Indian scientists—A.C. Mitra.
(INSDOC, 1969).
(Guide : S. Dutta). 718

Study of the citations appended to articles in Current Science, 1978-80—G. Dhanasekaran.
(Kamaraj University, 1981).
(Guide : A. Srimurugan). 719

Use of periodicals by research scholars : A study to recognise the pattern of use—T. Gopalakrishna.
(University of Madras, 1978). 720

Classification

Broad book classification for school libraries—A.R. Sethi.
(University of Delhi, 1981).
(Guide : Krishan Kumar). 721

Broad documentary classification—Bimal Kanti Sen.
(University of Delhi, 1983).
(Guide : Krishan Kumar). 722

Classificatory language and its application—Shreegopal Sharma.
(Vikram University, 1975).
(Guide : G.D. Bhargava). 723

Logical and hierarchical museum classification scheme—B.K. Chakraborty.
(INSDOC, 1975).
(Guide : T.N. Rajan). 724

Role of classification in mechanised information retrieval systems : A trend survey—J. Srihariraju.
(Punjab University, 1971). 725

Classification—Bibliographic classification

Critical evaluation of BC 2—Yogendra Singh.
(University of Delhi, 1983).
(Guide : Krishan Kumar). 726

Entry No.

Classification—Colon classification

Colon classification for macro documents in Library and Information Science—M. Santhanam. (University of Madras, 1982). 727

Colon classification for nutrition—N. Ushakumari. (University of Madras, 1983). 728

Depth classification of Genetics in CC—Dasari Prabhakar. (University of Delhi, 1983). (Guide : M.M. Kashyap). 729

Depth schedule for Home Science in CC—Sushmabala. (University of Delhi, 1982). (Guide : Krishan Kumar). 730

Depth schedule of CC for Linguistics—Kalpana Roy. (University of Delhi, 1983). (Guide : M.M. Kashyap). 731

Development of CC scheme—Iqbal Ahmed Siddiqui. (Vikram University, 1978). (Guide : G.D. Bhargava). 732

Physiology : Depth classification version—Manoranjan Mahapatra. (University of Delhi, 1977). (Guide : Krishan Kumar). 733

Study of theory of library classification with special emphasis on the CC.—P. Vijaykumari. (Andhra University, 1980). (Guide : K. Sarada). 734

Classification—CC and DC

Classification of biological literature : A comparison of schedules of CC and DC—G.K. Manjunath. (University of Mysore, 1980). (Guide : N.B. Pangannaya). 735

Comparative study of Botany schedule in CC and DC—Asharani. (Punjab University, 1978). 736

Comparative study of Economics schedule in CC and

Entry No.

DC—Sukanya Wig.
(Punjab University, 1978). 737

Comparative study of English literature schedule in DC and CC—Harmeet Kaur.
(Punjab University, 1979). 738

Comparative study of Fine Arts class in CC and DC—Mohinder Kaur.
(Punjab University, 1981). 739

Comparative study of Generalia class in CC and DC —Satnam Singh Batra.
(Punjab University, 1980). 740

Comparative study of Zoology in CC and DC—K.S. Rao.
(Punjab University, 1980). 741

Classification—CC and UDC

Comparative study of CC (Ed : 6) and UDC (BS : 1OOO A)—Madanmohan Sharma.
(Punjab University, 1972). 742

Classification--Common isolates

Study of common isolates—G. Padmavati.
(Andhra University, 1980).
(Guide : P. Somaraju). 743

Treatment of common isolates in CC, DC and UDC—Abha Shrivastava.
(Vikram University, 1981).
(Guide : G.D. Bhargava). 744

Classification—Contribution

American contribution to library classification--M.L. Pasrija.
(BHU, 1968). 745

British contribution to classification—N.H. Pawar.
(BHU, 1968). 746

Indian contribution to library classification—R.J. Upadhyaya.
(BHU, 1968). 747

Entry No.

Classification—DC

Analytical study of three schedules of DC (A study in commemoration of Dewey's Decimal Classification Centenary Year)—A.Y. Asundi.
(INSDOC, 1976).
(Guides : B. Guha and T.N. Rajan). 748

Comparative study of 18th and 19th editions of DC—Mohanraj Pradhan.
(University of Delhi, 1982).
(Guide : C.P. Vashishth). 749

Comparative study of 18th and 19th edition to DC : Social Sciences class—H.S. Amaruddin Ahamad.
(Andhra University, 1980).
(Guide : K. Sivareddy). 750

Comparative study of the DC, Ed 18 and 19—Manmohan Singh.
(Punjab University, 1981). 751

Dewey Decimal Classification—S.M. Tripathi.
(BHU, 1968). 752

Dewey Decimal Classification—Depth schedules—Library and Information Science—M. Suriya.
(University of Madras, 1983). 753

Dewey Decimal Classification through a decade : A comparative study—C.M. Premalatha.
(University of Mysore, 1982).
(Guide : N.B. Pangannaya). 754

Classification—DC Mathematics

Mathematics schedule : A comparative study of the 16th and 18th editions of the DDC—V. Vijayasudha.
(Andhra University, 1981).
(Guide : P. Somaraju). 755

Classification—DC Psychology

Psychology : Subject treatment in DDC from 16th to 19th edition—K. Pushpa.
(Andhra University, 1980).
(Guide : P. Somaraju). 756

Entry No.

Classification—DC and LC

Comparative study of Library of Congress and Decimal Classification schemes—Navjot Kaur. (Punjab University, 1972). 757

Classification—Design

Design of depth classification of animal husbandry : An experiment—K. Ramaswami. (INSDOC, 1965). (Guide : T.N. Rajan). 758

Classification—Faceted

Faceted classification—Fateh Bahadur. (BHU, 1968). 759

Faceted classification as indexing technique—Rupan A. Singh. (Punjab University, 1981). 760

Faceted classification in solid state physics : An experiment—G.T. Mirchandani. (INSDOC, 1966). (Guide : T.N. Rajan). 761

Classification—Fundamental Categories

Designing of a fundamental category Personality of Sociology of Colon Classification—Bhopal Dutt Sharma. (University of Delhi, 1975). (Guide : M.M. Kashyap). 762

Fundamental categories—T.M.K. Gandhi. (Vikram University, 1979). (Guide : S.S. Agrawal). 763

Classification—General vs. Special

General vs. special classifications—Anita Garg. (University of Rajasthan, 1977). 764

Entry No.

Classification—History

Development of classification schemes—Renu Chaddha. (University of Rajasthan, 1975). 765

History of library classification since 1876—S.S. Hallikeri. (Dharwar University, 1980). (Guide : Kumbhar). 766

Twentieth century developments in library classification—Daulat Jotwani. (University of Rajasthan, 1978). 767

Classification—Literature

Classification literature : Survey and trend, 1968-78—C. Nalinidevi. (BHU, 1979). 768

Classification—Notation

Development in notational technique, 1876 to Elsinore conference—M.P. Singh. (BHU, 1968). 769

Development of chemical notation systems—M.S. Naigonkar. (INSDOC, 1970). (Guide : B. Guha). 770

Notation in schemes of library classification : A review—Vedprakash Khare. (Vikram University, 1977). (Guide : G.D. Bhargava). 771

Classification—Research

Classification research in India—Kamla Shrivastava. (Vikram University, 1975). (Guide : G.D. Bhargava). 772

Research in library classification in India—Roshanlal Arora. (Punjab University, 1977). 773

Trend in classification research—R.N. Vashistha. (University of Rajasthan, 1977). 774

Entry No.

Classification—Systems

Analysis of current development of classification schemes in Library and Information systems—M.P. Sujatha.
(Bangalore University, 1979). 775

Classification systems—C.V. Rajan Pillai.
(BHU, 1973). 776

Classification—Thesaurus

Classification : A thesaurus—S. Rajendran.
(University of Mysore, 1982).
(Guide : N.B. Pangannaya). 777

Classification—UDC

Universal Decimal classification—P.K. Kaul.
(BHU, 1967). 778

Classification—UDC and LC

Comparative study of schedules of Social Sciences in UDC and LC—Sitaram Varma.
(Punjab University, 1974). 779

Classification and Cataloguing

Readers' approach to classification and cataloguing—R.M. Pandey.
(BHU, 1973). 780

Conference

Library conferences—G. Mishra.
(BHU, 1973). 781

Contact libraries

Survey of libraries of India's missions abroad with special reference to UK, USA and USSR—Asha Sood.
(Punjab University, 1972). 782

Entry No.

Co-operation

Cooperation among libraries in Bangalore—V. Srinivasan. (Bombay University, 1973). 783

Cooperation among the university and college libraries in Dharwar : A plan—V.S. Javaji. (Dharwar University, 1974). (Guide : Kumbhar). 784

Cooperation in libraries—Shikharani Bhattacharya. (University of Rajasthan, 1976). 785

Cooperative acquisition and cataloguing—V.K. Srivastava. (BHU, 1970). 786

Cooperative storage and acquisition in USA : A literature survey—Anuradha Mathur. (University of Rajasthan, 1979). 787

Inter-library loan—Amarjyoti Saxena. (Vikram University, 1978). (Guide : S. Kumar). 788

International cooperation in the field of Library and Information Science—N.J. Sebastian. (University of Delhi, 1977). (Guide : P.B. Mangla). 789

International library cooperation in academic libraries : Special reference to Nepal—Mridula Kulmi. (Punjab University, 1983). 790

Library resource sharing at national and international level—Roshan. (Punjab University, 1979). 791

Resource sharing among social science research libraries in Trivandrum city—A. Syamalakumari. (Kerala University, 1981). 792

Standardization for international cooperation : Universal Bibliographic Control (UBC)—A.G. Fernandez. (University of Rajasthan, 1979). 793

Entry No.

Documentation—Asia

Documentation on Asia : An operation manual—Shalini Rewadikar.
(University of Delhi, 1973).
(Guide : M.M. Kashyap). 794

Documentation—Bibliography

Documentation of bibliography : Subject bibliography and physical bibliography—M.V. Venugopal.
(BHU, 1966). 795

Documentation—Cataloguing

Documentation of cataloguing—S.K. Srivastava.
(BHU, 1966). 796

Documentation of dictionary catalogue—N.B. Joshi.
(BHU, 1966). 797

Documentation of subject cataloguing—Badriprasad.
(BHU, 1966). 798

Documentation on subject cataloguing—Dura Raina.
(BHU, 1972). 799

Documentation—Children's library

Documentation of children's library—S.K. Pandey.
(BHU, 1966). 800

Documentation—College library

Documentation on college libraries—P.L. Nuchanarth.
(BHU, 1972). 801

Documentation—Defence

Library resources and documentation services in Defence Research and Development Organization : A survey—S.K. Taneja.
(INSDOC, 1973).
(Guides : B. Guha and T.S. Rajagopalan). 802

Entry No.

Documentation—Documentation

Documentation of documentation—B.L. Chicken.
(BHU, 1966). 803

Documentation—Econometrics

Documentation of econometrics—Fateh Bahadur.
(BHU, 1968). 804

Documentation—Education

Documentation of education for librarianship—G.V.S.L. Narasimha Raju.
(BHU, 1972). 805

Documentation of education for special librarianship—T. Madhusudhanarao.
(BHU, 1972). 806

Documentation—History

Recent trends in documentation since 1970—G.L. Jat.
(University of Rajasthan, 1979). 807

Documentation—Humanities

Documentation centre for Humanities in India : A plan—Narinder Kaur.
(Punjab University, 1982). 808

Documentation sources in the field of Humanities with special reference to India : A literature survey and trend—Kista Reddy.
(BHU, 1979). 809

Documentation—India

Development of documentation in India—V.K. Maiwal.
(Vikram University, 1973).
(Guide : A. Tejomurty). 810

Documentation—Library building

Documentation of library building—S.K. Khare.
(BHU, 1966). 811

Entry No.

Documentation of library building—H.D. Mishra. (BHU, 1973). 812

Documentation—Library cooperation

Documentation on library cooperation—Ved Prakash. (BHU, 1966). 813

Documentation—Library development

Documentation on library development in under-developed countries in the sixties—S.P. Mukherjee. (BHU, 1970). 814

Documentation—Library movement

Documentation of library movement in India since independence—R.N. Singh. (BHU, 1970). 815

Documentation—Library services

Documentation of library service—S.P. Mehta. (BHU, 1966). 816

Documentation services in Indian libraries—O.P. Uppal. (BHU, 1976). 817

Documentation—Library system

Documentation of regional library systems in UK and USA—P.A. Namlao. (BHU, 1976). 818

Documentation on national library systems with a special reference to library set up in India—Rakesh Kumar. (BHU, 1973). 819

Documentation—Library techniques

Documentation on Indian library techniques—J.S. Tiwana. (BHU, 1966). 820

Entry No.

Documentation—Medicine

Medical documentation in India—P.E. Thomas.
(Bombay University, 1976). 821

Documentation—Paddy

Documentation list on paddy—Vijayprasad Rai.
(BHU, 1968). 822

Documentation—Phytopathology

Documentation of phytopathology—R.R. Deb.
(BHU, 1968). 823

Documentation—Public libraries

Documentation on public libraries—A.A.N. Raju.
(BHU, 1966). 824

Documentation—Reference service

Documentation of reference service—
Ajoy Mukhopadhyay.
(BHU, 1966). 825

Documentation—Research

Documentation research in India—Rajwant Singh.
(University of Rajasthan, 1975). 826

Documentation—Science

Documentation services in science and technology in India : An evaluative study—S.P. Singh.
(University of Delhi, 1976).
(Guide : P.B. Mangla). 827

Documentation work in a multi-discipline research laboratory : A case study on the Regional Research Laboratory, Bhubaneswar—
K. Subramanyam.
(INSDOC, 1967).
(Guide : T.S. Rajagopalan). 828

Entry No.

Documentation—Social Sciences

Documentation in social sciences with special reference to India—N.B. Pangannaya.
(BHU, 1968). 829

Documentation services in social sciences in India ; An evaluative study—Renu Chabbra.
(University of Delhi, 1976).
(Guide : P.B. Mangla). 830

Organisation of Social Science Documentation in India with reference to ICSSR—S. Srinivas.
(Dharwar University, 1979).
(Guide : M.R. Kumbhar). 831

Documentation—Universe of subjects

Documentation of universe of subjects : Its structure and development—D. Chandran.
(BHU, 1972). 832

Documentation—University libraries

Documentation on university library—S.N. Singh.
(BHU, 1966). 833

Documentation—World documentation centres

Documentation and library activities of Unesco—Chhabil Dass.
(BHU, 1974). 834

Documentation of world documentation centres—P.S. Kaeosri.
(BHU, 1970). 835

Education—Bibliography

Classified bibliography on library education, 1967-75—Manjurani Jain.
(University of Delhi, 1976).
(Guide : M.M. Kashyap). 836

Education—India

Continuing education for librarians : Current trends

Entry No.

and plan for India—R. Shivanna.
(Bangalore University, 1977). 837

Current trends in library science education in India—Ravindu Kaur.
(Punjab University, 1980). 838

Curriculum development for the Bachelor of Library Science in Indian universities—Raman Goel.
(Punjab University, 1983). 839

Development of library education in India with special reference to Master's degree course—R. Subbaiah.
(Vikram University, 1974).
(Guide : G.D. Bhargava). 840

Development of library science education in India in post-independence period : A survey—Ramarao.
(Punjab University, 1976). 841

Education for academic librarianship in India—A.K. Nath.
(University of Delhi, 1979).
(Guide : D.S. Aggarwal). 842

Education for librarianship and documentation training facilities in India—T.K. Manmohandas.
(BHU, 1974). 843

Education for librarianship in India—Kanwaljit Singh.
(BHU, 1968). 844

Education for librarianship through correspondence in India : Present status and future prospect—Ruby Batra.
(Punjab University, 1984). 845

Evolution, objectives and patterns in certificate course in library science in India : A study—Manohar Lal.
(Punjab University, 1972). 846

Library education in developing countries, with reference to India—Alka Agarwal.
(University of Rajasthan, 1978). 847

Library education in India—P.C. Jain.
(University of Rajasthan, 1978). 848

Library education in India : A study—Namita Kaula.

Entry No.

(Dharwar University, 1976).
(Guide : Kumbhar). 849

Library science course in government polytechnics in Punjab, Haryana and UP : A study—Sandeep Kaur.
(Punjab University, 1980). 850

Library science in India : A study of manpower and educational programmes—S.B. Ghosh.
(INSDOC, 1971).
(Guide : T.S. Rajagopalan). 851

Library training course of the Directorate of Libraries, Maharashtra—S.R. Natu.
(Poona University, 1982).
(Guide : M.R. Riswadkar). 852

Role of departments of library science in continuing education for librarians in India : A survey—Jagdish P. Verma.
(Punjab University, 1984). 853

Socio-economic survey of Master's graduates of department of library science, Punjab University, Chandigarh from 1970-71 to 1982-83—Harsharani Gupta.
(Punjab University, 1984). 854

Teaching of Master of Library Science in Indian universities—Radhakrishan Sapru.
(Punjab University, 1975). 855

Education—United Kingdom

History of library education in United Kingdom from 1900 to 1976—Ranjana Vohra.
(Punjab University, 1977). 856

Education—United States of America

History of library education in USA from 1900 to 1976—Rajpal Singh.
(Punjab University, 1977). 857

Survey of research made at the level of Ph.D. in the field of library science in USA from 1950-76—

Entry No.

K. Nanda.
(Punjab University, 1977). 858

Information Science

Acronyms and abbreviations in information science—
Neelam Gupta.
(University of Rajasthan, 1980). 859

Concept of information science in relation to library science : A paradigmatic study—
Virendra Kumar Anand.
(Punjab University, 1984). 860

Information science : Its structure and development—
N.S. Ashalatha.
(Bangalore University, 1977). 861

Information Science—Data bases

Bibliographical and non-bibliographical data bases : A comparative study—Meenakshi Sharma.
(Punjab University, 1984). 862

Importance of data bases in social sciences with reference to ICSSR—Kailash C. Das.
(University of Delhi, 1983).
(Guide : V.K. Sundaram). 863

Review of the literature on data bases—K. Subhashini.
(INSDOC, 1974).
(Guide : T.N. Rajan). 864

Information Science—Literature

Library and information science literature in the fifties : A survey and trend—Radharao.
(BHU, 1979). 865

Library and information science literature in the seventies : A survey and trend—Ganga Shime.
(BHU, 1979). 866

Library and information science literature : Literature survey and trend, 1960-69—R. Ramachandran.
(BHU, 1979). 867

Entry No.

Information Science—Information dissemination

Brief review of SDI services—H.K. Sampathu.
(INSDOC, 1974).
(Guide : T.N. Rajan). 868

Communication behaviour of scientists in universities —K.R. Geetha.
(University of Mysore, 1980).
(Guide : R. Shalini). 869

Current awareness service : A study— R. Satyanarayana.
(INSDOC, 1966).
(Guide : B. Guha). 870

Development and implementation of a working model of manual SDI services in an academic library— P. Nirmaladevi.
(SNDT Women's University, 1982). 871

Proposal for SDI services for the centre of advanced studies in biochemistry : Indian Institute of Science, Bangalore—Hemalata Iyer.
(Bangalore University, 1975) 872

SDI service for the research scholars of the department of Physics in the University of Cochin : A pilot study and plan—P. Thankappan.
(University of Madras, 1982). 873

Study of effectiveness of the current contents in physical and chemical, life sciences and engineering and technology sections— M.P. Narappareddy.
(Bangalore University, 1978). 874

Information science—Information retrieval

Application of punched cards to library routines and information retrieval : A trend report, 1960-64— J.K. Ahluwalia.
(INSDOC, 1965).
(Guide : A.S. Raizada). 875

Computerized data retrieval : An experiment with IBM 1620—L.J. Haravu.

Entry No.

(INSDOC, 1965)
(Guide : A.S. Raizada). 876

Information retrieval and reprography—R.N. Kaul.
(BHU, 1967). 877

Manuscript information storage and retrieval system in the Government Oriental Manuscripts Library, Madras : A case study—R. Manivannan.
(University of Madras, 1983). 878

Mechanized information retrieval from abstracts literature in chemical engineering using IBM 1620—D.S.R. Murty.
(INSDOC, 1969).
(Guide : A.S. Raizada). 879

Semi-automatic system of information storage and retrieval applied to IAEA Directory of World Nuclear Reactors—N.M. Malwad.
(INSDOC, 1966).
(Guide : A.S. Raizada). 880

System's approach to the optional number of profiles based on the user's capacity—N. Rajagopalan.
(INSDOC, 1976).
(Guide : H.N. Mahabala). 881

Testing comparison and evaluation of information retrieval systems—G.N. Salvi.
(INSDOC, 1968).
(Guide : T.N. Rajan). 882

Information science—Information requirements, Economics

Information needs of nationalised banks—N.M. Ghaisas.
(SNDT Women's University, 1983). 883

Information seeking behaviour of persons in an industrial establishment : A case study—A. Meenakshi.
(Andhra University, 1981).
(Guide : G.V.L.N. Raju). 884

Entry No.

Information science—Information requirements, Engineering

Information needs of engineering scientists in CSIR Madras complex—Abbas Ibrahim. (University of Madras, 1982). 885

Information needs of engineering scientists in India—B.N. Singh. (BHU, 1978). 886

Information science—Information requirements, Food

Information uses and needs of food scientists : A case study of CFTRI, Mysore—Sunil Kumar Trivedi. (University of Mysore, 1983). (Guide : B.S. Maheswarappa). 887

Information science—Information requirements, Linguistics

Information requirements of the linguists : A case study of CIIL, Mysore—K.V. Lakshminarasamma. (University of Mysore, 1982). (Guide : H.A. Khan). 888

Information science—Information requirements, Medicine

Information needs of medical personnel in Madras city —R. Rukmini. (University of Madras, 1981). 889

Information scicnce—Information requirements, Physics

Information and documentary needs of the researchers in physics at Ahmedabad—S.A. Majumdar. (SNDT Women's University, 1983). 890

Information science—Information requirements, Research scholars

Information gathering habits of research workers :

Entry No.

A survey—S.G. Bhatt.
(Bombay University, 1971). 891

Information Science—Information requirements, Science

Approach to information by the research scholars in science in Karnataka University library—S.L. Sangam.
(Dharwar University, 1978).
(Guide : Kumbhar). 892

Information needs, habits problems and awareness of scientists in an Indian university : A study—Baldev Singh.
(Punjab University, 1982). 893

Information requirements of the faculty and research scholars of Indian Institute of Science, Bangalore—M.G. Lakshmanaswamy.
(Bangalore University, 1979). 894

Information Science—Information requirements, Social Sciences.

Information requirements of the Social Science research scholars at BHU—Anju Agrawal.
(BHU, 1976). 895

Study of documentary needs of sociologists in four institutions in Bombay—G.G. Pandey.
(SNDT Women's University, 1983). 896

Information Science—Information requirements, Synthetics

Information needs and services in J.K. Synthetics, Kota ; Gwalior Rayons, Gwalior : A survey—N.C. Boonlia.
(Vikram University, 1977).
(Guide : A. Tejomurty). 897

Entry No.

**Information science—
Information requirements, Teachers**

Information seeking behaviour of Bangalore university teachers and research scholars—T.V. Venkataramaniah. (BHU, 1976). 898

Information services

Library and information services in the PGI library Chandigarh, A study—Renu Thakar. (Punjab University, 1982). 899

Information services—Agriculture

Information activities in the field of agriculture and veterinary sciences in India : Survey and trend—Jagdish Narayan Sharma. (BHU, 1979). 900

Information services in agricultural sciences—Lalta Singh. (BHU, 1979). 901

Use of reading materials by research scholars and PG students in the university of agricultural sciences library of Karnataka : A survey—S.R. Hiremath. (Dharwar University, 1977). (Guide : Kumbhar). 902

Information services—Business

Planning of library and information services of a business management library—Neeru. (Punjab University, 1982). 903

Information services—Chemistry

Information and communication in chemistry—Shailendra Kaushik. (University of Delhi, 1981). (Guide : J.L. Sardana). 904

Patterns of literature use by the scientists at the NCL, Pune—M.B. Patil.

Entry No.

(Poona University, 1982).
(Guide : M.R. Riswadkar). 905

Information services—Economics

Information use : A survey of the staff and researchers of the department of economics, Andhra University, Waltair—S. Indira.
(Andhra University, 1980).
(Guide : B. Vijayalakshmi). 906

Information services—Electronics

Electronics information access—S.N. Karkhanis.
(INSDOC, 1971).
(Guide : T.N. Rajan). 907

Information services—India

Computerized information services with special reference to India : A study—Kiran Ahuja.
(Punjab University, 1974). 908

Efforts and programmes of ICSSR, CSIR and Department of Science and Technology for the development of Library and Information Services in India—A.S. Gupta.
(University of Delhi, 1977).
(Guide : P.B. Mangla). 909

Information services—Industry

Industrial information service in India (Coal, steel, cement and fertilizer) : A survey project—Suryanath Singh.
(BHU, 1979). 910

Information services—Mathematics

Ballistics : A biblioview : Ballistics information and its organisation for retrieval and dissemination—O.J. Narayana.
(Bombay University, 1976). 911

Entry No.

Information services—Medicine

Approach to information by research workers in medical sciences—G.P. Singh.
(BHU, 1971). 912

Information services in medical libraries with special reference to India—A.B. Gupta.
(BHU. 1976). 913

Use of periodical literature in medical college libraries of Bombay—Minaxi N. Bhatt.
(SNDT Women's University, 1981).
(Guide : M.K.R. Naidu). 914

Information services—Physics

Information use by physicists : A case study at Andhra university—L. Ramaswami Sarma.
(Andhra University, 1981).
(Guide : B. Vijayalakshmi). 915

Information services—Politics

Planning of library and information services in the Punjab Vidhan Sabha library—Kanwaljit Kaur.
(Punjab University, 1981). 916

Information services—Radioastronomy.

Survey of information services in radioastronomy—Y.M. Patil.
(INSDOC, 1978).
(Guide : V.R. Venugopal). 917

Information services—Railways

Technical information services for Indian railways—K.S. Sivaraman.
(INSDOC, 1970).
(Guide : T.S. Rajagopalan). 918

Information services—Sciences

Bibliographical services of INSDOC : An analytical study for the period 1968-70—S.P. Gulati.

Entry No.

(INSDOC, 1971).
(Guide : O.N. Chaddga). 919

Readers' services in scientific and technical research institutional libraries in Bombay—T.N. Patil.
(Dharwar University, 1978).
(Guide : Kumbhar). 920

Science information services in CSIR laboratories and cooperative research associations : A referral directory—R.L. Anand.
(INSDOC, 1974).
(Guide : T.S. Rajagopalan). 921

Use of photopathology literature by Indian scientists : A bibliometric study—S.K. Bose.
(BHU, 1978). 922

Utilization of Soviet scientific information in India through periodicals—S.S. Murty.
(INSDOC, 1970).
(Guide : T.S. Rajagopalan). 923

Information services—Social sciences

Information services in social sciences (with special reference to abstracting and indexing)—C.S.S.P. Sastry.
(INSDOC, 1978).
(Guide : B.K. Sen). 924

Research and bibliographical activities in social science research institutions in India—Rachna Malhotra.
(Punjab University, 1983). 925

Information services—Technology

Personalised information services in CLRI, Madras : An assessment—N. Raghavan.
(University of Madras, 1983). 926

Study of the use of monographs at the CLRI library, Madras—Y. Meenabhavani.
(University of Madras, 1983). 927

Use of monographs in the central library, IIT,

Entry No.

Madras—Anita Rajabhooshanam.
(University of Madras, 1982). 928

Information services—Uganda

Perspective planning of information services in Uganda—R. Ogwang-Ameny.
(INSDOC, 1978).
(Guide : T.S. Rajagopalan). 929

Information services—Veterinary science

Relevance of periodicals acquired by the college of veterinary and animal sciences of Kerala Agricultural University : A study—K.S. Ambili.
(Kerala University, 1982). 930

Information sources—Agriculture

Control and dissemination of unpublished information in the field of agriculture—S. Moitra.
(INSDOC, 1969).
(Guide : T.S. Rajagopalan). 931

Documentary sources of information in agricultural science—R.D. Mehta.
(University of Rajasthan, 1979). 932

Sources of information in Indian agriculture : A survey project—S. Ch. Rath.
(BHU, 1979). 933

Information sources—Biology

Evaluation of information sources in mariculture in CMFRI library—E. Johnson.
(University of Madras, 1981). 934

Use of sources of information by Ph.D. students in Zoology and Botany for 1972-75 in Rajasthan University—Mukesh Kumar Sharma.
(University of Rajasthan, 1980). 935

Information sources—Chemistry

Assessment of the adequacy of information sources in

Entry No.

bio-chemistry in the university of Madras library —V. Kasirao.
(University of Madras, 1982). 936

Information sources—Engineering

Highway engineering : A perspective and sources of information—Krishan Kumar.
(INSDOC, 1978).
(Guide : M.C. Raghavan). 937

Information sources—Films

Assessment and evaluation of information sources for film libraries—Saral Kane.
(Poona University, 1981).
(Guide : M.R. Riswadkar). 938

Information sources—History

Availability and uses of information sources of Indian History (British period) at Mysore university library—Ramesh Gandhi.
(University of Mysore, 1983).
(Guide : H.A. Khan). 939

Information sources—Industry

Newspaper as source of industrial information : An analytical study—Mohmed Tahir.
(University of Mysore, 1978).
(Guide : R. Shalini). 940

Information sources—Law

Indian legal sources of information : An evaluation—Satish Chander.
(University of Delhi, 1981).
(Guide : C.P. Vashisth). 941

Information sources—Literature

Sources of information used by the research scholars in Tamil literature and Tamil linguistics : A

Entry No.

bibliographic analysis—C.N. Thilagavathy.
(University of Madras, 1983). 942

Information sources—Mass communication

Information sources on mass communication : A guide —B.K. Prasad
(INSDOC, 1974).
(Guides : T.N. Rajan and B. Guha). 943

Information sources—Medicine

Sources of information used by post-graduate surgery students : a bibliometric study—Venkataraman Bharathi.
(University of Madras, 1981). 944

Use of information sources by faculty in medical college libraries in Rajasthan.
(University of Rajasthan, 1979). 945

Information sources—Physics

Renewable energy information sources and services in Gujarat : A review—P.J. Pathak.
(SNDT Women's University, 1983). 946

Information sources—Psychology

Study of information sources in Psychology—Balakrishna Acharya.
(University of Mysore, 1983).
(Guide : N.B. Pangannaya). 947

Information sources—Public health

Guide to information sources in public health engineering—S.K. Kesharwani.
(INSDOC, 1969).
(Guidc : B. Guha). 948

Information sources—Science

Newspaper as a source of scientific and technical information : An analytical study—

Entry No.

O.R. Manoramaraju.
(University of Madras, 1980). 949

Sources consulted in research dissertations : A comparative study on the patterns of usage of source materials in Ph.D. theses in plant science and animal science—R. Paulmohan Roy.
(University of Madras, 1978). 950

Information sources—Sociology

Abstracts of M. Phil. and Ph.D. dissertations in sociology submitted to Punjab University—Kumudlata.
(Punjab University, 1983). 951

Information sources—Technology

Guide to information sources in leather science and technology—V.S. Padmanabhan.
(INSDOC, 1967).
(Guide : S. Parthasarathy). 952

Information system

Information support for government decision-making and planning : A blue print for an information system for Uttar Pradesh Secretariat—R.K. Mehrotra.
(INSDOC, 1978).
(Guide : T.S. Rajagopalan). 953

Information system—Agriculture

AGRIS and INIS : A comparative study—Durgesh Nandini.
(Punjab University, 1984). 954

Organisation of information transfer systems in agriculture with particular reference to India—Haradhan Bose.
(University of Delhi, 1981).
(Guide : Krishan Kumar). 955

Planning an agricultural information system for

Entry No.

India—Harbhajan Singh.
(Punjab University, 1981). 956

Information system—Asia

Proposed plan for a biomedical library and information network in the south-east Asia region—K. Thet Htar.
(University of Delhi, 1979).
(Guide : V.K. Sundaram). 957

Information system—Biology

Information system for biological sciences : A proposed model for India—Meena Khurana.
(Punjab University, 1982). 958

Information system—Buddhism

Information system in Buddhism : Literature survey and trend—Pharmaha Thaworu Foofuang.
(BHU, 1979). 959

Information system—Economics

Marketing information system : A diagnostic study—Ansa Elizabeth Verghese.
(University of Madras, 1982). 960

Information system—Education

National information system in education for India: A plan—Sunderlal Verma.
(University of Delhi, 1982).
(Guide : J.L. Sardana). 961

Information system—Engineering

Information system and services to the scientists of the Combat Vehicle Research and Development Establishment : A system study and issues—K. Narayanaswamy.
(University of Madras, 1982). 962

National information centre for heavy electrical

Entry No.

engineering : A proposed plan—
J. Indira Subbaram.
(INSDOC, 1974).
(Guide : T.S. Rajagopalan). 963

Information system—Geology

Planning a geo-science information system for India—
Gurdial Chand.
(Punjab University, 1982). 964

Information system—India

Information management in India : A literature survey
—Baman Parida.
(Vikram University, 1983).
(Guide : G.D. Bhargava). 965

Information system in India : Survey and trend—
Arunkumar Sinha.
(BHU, 1979). 966

Information system for the Indian parliament—
Manmohan Lal.
(INSDOC, 1978).
(Guide : B. Guha). 967

National information system—Rupendra.
(University of Rajasthan, 1979). 968

National information system : Literature survey—
Abha Kumar.
(Vikram University, 1979).
(Guide : A. Tejomurty). 969

National scientific information centres of India—
Pawan Kumar Gupta.
(University of Delhi, 1976).
(Guide : V.K. Sundaram). 970

Information system—Medicine

Medical information system : A literature survey—
P.C. Gupta.
(University of Rajasthan, 1979). 971

Entry No.

Information system—Nuclear science

Major nuclear information handling centres in the world with particular reference to the development of International Nuclear Information System —M.K. Dhirendrarao.
(INSDOC, 1978).
(Guides : V.A. Kamath and M.K. Raghavendrarao). 972

Information system—Science

Development of infrastructure for national information system for science and technology in India— S. Devarajamma.
(Bangalore University, 1977). 973

Information network for science and technology in Trivandrum—R. Prasannakumari.
(Kerala University, 1982). 974

Information system—Technology

Technical information system : A blueprint for BHEL, Boiler plant unit, Tiruchirapalli— T. R. Ananthasankar.
(INSDOC, 1965).
(Guide : T.S. Rajagopalan). 975

Information system—USA

Information system of the National Library of Medicine (USA), Chemical Abstracts Service and the American Institute of Physics : A comparative study—Purnimadevi Thakur.
(Punjab University, 1984). 976

Information system—World

Global information system : A literature survey— Neelam Taneja.
(University of Rajasthan, 1981). 977

International information network—S. B. Malik.
(University of Rajasthan, 1977). 978

Survey of global information networks—

Entry No.

B. Zaman Khan.
(INSDOC, 1978).
(Guide : T.N. Rajan). 979

UNISIST : A study—Baldev Dass.
(Punjab University, 1981). 980

UNISIST : Its role in the development of information system—Shyamoli Chatterjee.
(University of Delhi, 1976).
(Guide : P.B. Mangla). 981

Information technology

Communication of scientific and technological information in India : A perspective study—A. Srimurugan.
(Dharwar University, 1978).
(Guide : Kumbhar). 982

Information technology and its impact on the present day libraries and their users—Aya Singh.
(Punjab University, 1984). 983

Libraries

Knowledge : Its communication and the libraries—B.L. Gupta.
(University of Rajasthan, 1976). 984

Libraries—Directory

Directory of libraries and librarians of Jaipur—Gulshan Kumar.
(University of Rajasthan, 1980). 985

Libraries—India

Book trade and libraries in Bombay—T.M. Sheth.
(SNDT Women's University, 1984). 986

Development of libraries in Manipur—Naoram Giridhari Singh.
(Punjab University, 1982).

Impact of Five-Year Plans on library development in India—Joginder Singh.
(Punjab University, 1974). 988

Entry No.

Impact of Indian publishing trade on the development of libraries in the post-independence days—Rama Sharma. (Punjab University, 1975). 989

Importance of libraries in changing concept of education after independence—Shil Kumar Jindal. (Punjab University, 1977). 990

Libraries in medieval India—R.R. Atgur. (Bombay University, 1974). 991

Role of libraries in implementing the 20 point programme of our Prime Minister, Indira Gandhi—Moirangthem Choaba Singh. (Punjab University, 1984). 992

Survey of popular libraries in Kerala—P. Vasudevan. (Bombay University, 1971). 993

Libraries—Nepal

Growth of education and its influence for the advancement of libraries in Nepal after the revolution of 1951—Madhusudan. (Punjab University, 1980). 994

Library profession—Bibliography

Bibliography of Ranganathan, 1962-82—O.P. Singh. (Vikram University, 1983). (Guide : S.S. Agrawal). 995

Library profession—Biography

Ranganathan : A genius and master architect of library Profession in India—B.B. Shukla. (BHU, 1975). 996

Library profession—India

Changing concept of librarianship in the post-independence period in India—Mohinder Mohan Rastogi. (Punjab University, 1975). 997

Entry No.

Current trades in library profession in India : Its survey—Manjit Kaur.
(Punjab University, 1979). 998

Librarianship and social change in India : 1947 to present—Madhu Saini.
(Punjab University, 1983). 999

Librarianship in India and abroad : Retrospect and prospect—G.D. Bhargava.
(Vikram University, 1976).
(Guide : S.S. Agrawal). 1000

Six year work in Indian librarianship 1970-75—M.L. Vishalakshi.
(University of Mysore, 1978).
(Guide : H.A. Khan). 1001

Library profession—Job satisfaction

Job satisfaction among library personnel of school and college libraries in Ujjain city—Anjali Mungee.
(Vikram University, 1980).
(Guide : A. Tejomurty). 1002

Job satisfaction of professional librarians of special libraries in Delhi—Padmaja D. Alurkar.
(Vikram University, 1983).
(Guide : G.D. Bhargava). 1003

Library profession—Personnel

Library personnel—R.S. Sharma.
(BHU, 1967). 1004

Library profession—Status

Academic status for professional staff of university libraries—U.S.A. and India—Mohindra Singh Sidhu.
(University of Delhi, 1974).
(Guide : P.B. Mangla). 1005

Status and service conditions of librarians in academic libraries of Delhi—B.R. Kanwal.
(BHU, 1974). 1006

Entry No.

Status and service conditions of college librarians in Andhra Pradesh—P.S.G. Kumar. (BHU, 1971). 1007

Status and service conditions of college librarians in Bihar—R.S. Tiwari. (BHU, 1971). 1008

Status of librarians in a special library with special reference to India : A study—Gurdeep Singh Dhillon. (Punjab University, 1976). 1009

University librarian (A study of his status and role)—B.S. Saini. (Punjab University, 1972). 1010

Library profession—Women

Women in librarianship with special reference to India —Sumati. (Punjab University, 1982). 1011

Women professional librarians : A case study—H.S. Parekh. (Bombay University, 1977). 1012

Women workers in libraries—Shashi. (Punjab University, 1979). 1013

Library relations

Public relation in libraries—J.M. Rathore. (University of Rajasthan, 1978). 1014

Library science—Bibliography

Bibliographical control of library and information science literature in India : A state of the art study —Kulwant Kaur. (Punjab University, 1984). 1015

Survey of library science literature (Books of Ist edition only) published during 1965-75—Renu Sharma. (Punjab University, 1978). 1016

Library science— Contribution

Bowker and the library world—G. Suryarao.

Entry No.

(Andhra University, 1981).
(Guide : G.V.S.L.N. Raju). 1017

Contribution of Allen Kent in the field of librarianship and documentation—Surinder Kumar.
(Punjab University, 1977). 1018

Contribution of Andrew Carnegie (1835-1919) to library profession throughout the world—Priyadarshan Chaudhary.
(Punjab University, 1977). 1019

Contribution of B.C. Vickery towards modern librarianship—Inderdev.
(Punjab University, 1977). 1020

Contribution of Charles Ammi Cutter (1837-1903) to the field of library science—Ramesh Pal.
(Punjab University, 1977). 1021

Contribution of Henry Bliss to library profession—Harprem Lal Singh.
(Punjab University, 1974). 1022

Contribution of James Duff Brown (1862-1914) to the field of library science—Inder Vir.
(Punjab University, 1977). 1023

Contribution of Jesse H. Shera in the field of librarianship and documentation—S.C. Gandhi.
(Punjab University, 1971). 1024

Contribution of Lion Roy McColvin (1896-1976) to the field of library science—Jatinder Singh Bhandari.
(Punjab University, 1978). 1025

Contribution of Melvil Dewey : Literature survey—Amar Singh Yadav.
(University of Rajasthan, 1980). 1026

Contribution of R.R. Bowkar and Company to the field of library science—Madhubala.
(Punjab University, 1980). 1027

Contribution of R.R. Bowkar towards the field of library science—M.B. Chawla.
(Punjab University, 1971). 1028

Contribution of Ralph R. Shaw to the field of library

Entry No.

science—Ranjit Singh.
(Punjab University, 1977). 1029

Contribution of S.R. Ranganathan to the field of library science—Promila.
(Punjab University, 1973). 1030

Contribution of UGC towards the betterment of library science facilities in India—Urmila Gupta.
(Punjab University, 1973). 1031

Contribution of W.C. Berwick Sayers to library profession—Ashalata Gadru.
(Punjab University, 1974). 1032

Impact of S.R. Ranganathan's death on library science in India—Parmod Kumar Goyal.
(Punjab University, 1975). 1033

India's contribution to the field of library science after 1947 : A study—Raghubir Singh Dang.
(Punjab University, 1976). 1034

Unesco's contribution to documentation, libraries and archives—M.V.D' Souza.
(University of Rajasthan, 1979). 1035

Library science—Literature

Bibliometric analysis of the structure of the literature of library science—T.S. Ramakrishnan.
(University of Madras, 1980). 1036

Growth and development of library science literature in India from 1913 : A survey—
Chandershekhar Kalia.
(Punjab University, 1983). 1037

Library science—Periodicals

Comparative study of periodical literature in library science in India and U.K. (1976-80)—
B.M. Meera.
(University of Mysore, 1982).
(Guide : H.A. Khan). 1038

Content analysis of library science periodical literature published in India—B.A. Mokashi.
(SNDT Women's University, 1984). 1039

Entry No.

Price trend in library science journals—M. Anuradha. (Andhra University, 1981). (Guide : K. Sarada). 1040

Survey of library science periodicals in U.S.A., U.K., and India during the last one hundred years—Santosh Bakshi. (Punjab University, 1977). 1041

Library science—Research

Research methods in library and information science : A literature review—B. Saibaba. (University of Mysore, 1981). (Guide : N.B. Pangannaya). 1042

Library services

Impact of steep rise of price on library services—Kuldip Kumar Kalia. (Punjab University, 1974). 1043

Library services in India with slant to Jammu and Kashmir since 1960—Santosh Kumar Rawal. (Punjab University, 1974). 1044

Survey of library services in Himachal Pradesh—L.P. Sharma. (BHU, 1971). 1045

Survey of library services in Tirupathi town—G. Hemasundara Naidu. (Andhra University, 1980). (Guide : G.V.S.L.N. Raju). 1046

Library standards

Study of Indian library standards—H. Chaturvedi. (University of Rajasthan, 1978). 1047

Management

Impact of the non-book materials on the present day library organisation, administration and service—Upinder Kumar Tikku. (Punjab University, 1971). 1048

Entry No.

Organisation of non-book materials in libraries—Faizur Rahman.
(University of Delhi, 1964). 1049

Structural analysis of the literature of R & D management—M.P.K. Nagpal.
(INSDOC, 1979).
(Guide : B. Guha). 1050

Management—Acquisition

Acquisition in libraries—K.K. Kamal.
(BHU, 1967). 1051

Acquisition of reading materials in the university libraries of Maharashtra : A study—A.S. Mutekar.
(Dharwar University, 1976).
(Guide : Kumbhar). 1052

Document acquisition policies and procurement with special reference to university libraries of Gujarat —E.R.J. Christie.
(Vikram University, 1975).
(Guide : S. Kumar). 1053

Policies, procedures and problems of document procurement in the university libraries of Punjab and Union Territory of Chandigarh—Sukhvinder Singh.
(Punjab University, 1983). 1054

Price increase in periodicals : An investigation into the pattern of price variation and problems arising there from with suggestions for possible solutions —V. Ramakrishnan.
(Kerala University, 1981). 1055

Procurement of foreign periodicals through agents and by direct subscription : A comparative study based on cost benefit analysis of operations involved—Rosamma Joseph.
(Kerala University, 1982). 1056

Study of the acquisition policy and programme of the Mysore university library—Rajgopal.

Entry No.

(University of Mysore, 1977).
(Guide : T.V. Subramanyam). 1057

System analysis of the acquisition procedure of the Indian Institute of Science library Bangalore—M. Muralidharan.
(SNDT Women's University, 1981).
(Guide : H. Sales Pontes). 1058

Management—Book selection

Book selection in library—C.K. Sharma.
(BHU, 1970). 1059

Management—Circulation

Circulation systems—A. Chakraborty.
(BHU, 1967). 1060

Management—Maintenance

Maintenance of books and periodicals in libraries : Literature survey—C.B. Upadhyaya.
(University of Rajasthan, 1980). 1061

Management—Personnel

Frustration and extroversion-introversion : An inferential investigation of professional staff between Delhi University and JNU libraries—Lokesh Sharma.
(University of Delhi, 1984).
(Guide : J.L. Sardana). 1062

Library personnel in Punjab : A bio-bibliographical study—Joginder Pal.
(Punjab University, 1984). 1063

Personnel administration of Jawaharlal Nehru Krishi Viswavidyalaya library, Jabalpur—Mamta Shrivastava.
(Vikram University, 1981).
(Guide : S.S. Agrawal). 1064

Personnel management in city central library, Hubli : A survey—B.D. Kumbhar.

Entry No.

(Dharwar University, 1983).
(Guide : Kumbhar). 1065

Personnel management in the university libraries in Karnataka : A survey—K.V. Uma.
(Dharwar University, 1982).
(Guide : Kumbhar). 1066

State librarians of Punjab, Haryana and Himachal Pradesh, 1947-82 : A study of their roles as a leader in the library development in the State—Laxman Dhara Negi.
(Punjab University, 1984). 1067

Survey of job satisfaction and personality traits of Indian librarians—Ajit Singh.
(Punjab University, 1974). 1068

Management—Preservation

Deteriorating agents of library materials—Manpreet Kaur.
(Punjab University, 1981). 1069

Preservation of documents in libraries—B. Krupanjali.
(University of Madras, 1981). 1070

Problems of mutilation and loss of books in the libraries and their solution—Hari Pratap Singh.
(Punjab University, 1978). 1071

Management—Processing

Technical processing costs in academic libraries : A case study—V.K. Jain.
(INSDOC, 1971).
(Guide : A.S. Raizada). 1072

Treatment of periodical publications in a university and a technical library : A comparative study of time and cost analysis—Vishnu Kumar Mathur.
(Vikram University, 1977).
(Guide : S. Kumar). 1073

Treatment of non-book materials in libraries : Technical processing and storage—J.S. Arora.
(BHU, 1970). 1074

Entry No.

Management—Procurement

Document procurement service : An analytical study of the service rendered by INSDOC during the year 1963—E.H. Patnaik.
(INSDOC, 1969).
(Guide : M.L. Kachroo). 1075

Management—Space

Space management of Jayakar library in the year 2001 A.D.—A.N. Rasal.
(Poona University, 1982).
(Guide : M.R. Riswadkar). 1076

Organisations

Role of international and national organisations in the development of librarianship—C.B. Bharadwaj.
(University of Rajasthan, 1976). 1077

Public libraries

Libraries as media of communication—Shabad Kapur.
(Punjab University, 1979). 1078

Library and the community—A.K. Agrawal.
(University of Rajasthan, 1978). 1079

Mobile libraries—Lata Rao.
(BHU, 1967). 1080

Public library in twentieth century—Anirudh Prasad.
(BHU, 1968). 1081

Standards of public library service in U.S.A., U.K., and India since second world war : A literature survey—H.H. Pathak.
(University of Delhi, 1964). 1082

Public libraries—Andhra Pradesh

Development of Andhra Pradesh public libraries since 1960—A. Tarabai.
(University of Madras, 1979). 1083

Public library network of Visakhapatnam urban area : A survey—C. Sasikala.

Entry No.

(Andhra University, 1981).
(Guide : K. Sarada). 1084

Public library services in Andhra Pradesh—
N.R. Satyanarayana.
(BHU, 1971). 1085

Regional libraries in Andhra Pradesh : A study—
Sriramamurty.
(Dharwar University, 1976).
(Guide : Kumbhar). 1086

Public libraries—Assam

Evaluation of public library services in Assam—
P. Purkayastha.
(BHU, 1972). 1087

Public libraries—Chandigarh

Central State Library, Chandigarh : A study—Sushma.
(Punjab University, 1980). 1088

Public libraries—Delhi

Delhi public library—G.M. Ahuja.
(BHU, 1977). 1089

Delhi public library children section : Survey—
A.S. Alqazi.
(University of Delhi, 1972).
(Guide : B.V.R. Rao). 1090

Evaluation of the services provided by circulation and reference sections of Delhi public library—
Harikrishna Narayan.
(University of Delhi, 1978).
(Guide : D.S. Aggarwal). 1091

Public libraries—Extension service

Extension services in libraries in U.S.A.—
If the Kharurrisa.
(University of Rajasthan, 1978). 1092

Extension work in public libraries : A study—
I.H. Jahagirdar.

Entry No.

(Dharwar University, 1976).
(Guide : Kumbhar). 1093

Library extension service—D.D. Kapil.
(BHU, 1967). 1094

Public libraries—Gujarat

Administrative and financial position of public libraries in Gujarat State—P.V. Mehta.
(Punjab University, 1973). 1095

Public libraries—Haryana

District libraries in Haryana : A study—Satpal Singh.
(Punjab University, 1983). 1096

Public libraries—Himachal Pradesh

Planning a public library network in Kinnaur district (Himachal Pradesh)—C.V. Negi.
(Punjab University, 1981). 1097

Public libraries—India

Development of public libraries in India—M.R. Rawtani.
(University of Rajasthan, 1977). 1098

Evaluation of public libraries in India from earliest times to present day with special emphasis on British and independent India—J.K. Grewal.
(Punjab University, 1971). 1099

Public library system in India since independence—Balbir Kaur Khanuja.
(Vikram University, 1974).
(Guide : A. Tejomurty). 1100

Public libraries—Karnataka

Case study of origin and development of State Central Library, Bangalore—D. Shankarappa.
(University of Mysore, 1973).
(Guide : H.A. Khan). 1101

City central library, Hubli : A development plan—

Entry No.

S.H. Chandangoudar.
(Dharwar University, 1982).
(Guide : Kumbhar). 1102

Financial resources of the department of public libraries in Karnataka : A study—B.B. Hosamani.
(Dharwar University, 1983).
(Guide : Kumbhar). 1103

Karnataka State Central Library : A development plan—P.S. Kanamadi.
(Dharwar University, 1977).
(Guide : Kumbhar). 1104

Library development plan for Dharwar district, —S.R. Ijari.
(Dharwar University, 1972).
(Guide : Kumbhar). 1105

M.J. Pustakalaya : A development plan—C.M. Bhaiya.
(Dharwar University, 1975).
(Guide : Kumbhar). 1106

Mysore city central library : Past, present and future—N.S. Dasgarathy.
(University of Mysore, 1972).
(Guide : P.K. Patil). 1107

Public library system in Bijapur : A development plan—D.B. Minajagi.
(Dharwar University, 1976).
(Guide : Kumbhar). 1108

Readers' services in district central libraries in Karnataka State—V.K. Koti.
(Dharwar University, 1981).
(Guide : Kumbhar). 1109

Public libraries—Kerala

Evaluation of the role of local bodies in India in public library development and proposals for new directions with particular reference to Kerala—Joseph Kurien Pulikuthiel.
(Kerala University, 1982). 1110

Entry No.

Public libraries—Legislation

Assessment of public libraries' achievements after the enactment of Madras Public Libraries Act 1948 with special reference to Coimbatore district—K. Balasubramanyam.
(University of Mysore, 1978).
(Guide : H.A. Khan). 1111

Delivery of books and newspapers (Public Libraries) Act 1954 and its implementation in the Connemara (State Central) Public Library, Madras—A.M. Sundararajan.
(University of Madras, 1979). 1112

History of library legislation in India—Neelam Kungir.
(University of Rajasthan, 1978). 1113

Kerala Public Libraries Bill, 1971 : An evaluation—K. Ravindra Asari.
(University of Mysore, 1974).
(Guide : H.A. Khan). 1114

Library legislation—C.C. Bhandari.
(BHU, 1967). 1115

Library legislation in Himachal Pradesh—Sudarshan Kumar.
(Punjab University, 1982). 1116

Library legislation in India : A study—I.S. Hiremath.
(Dharwar University, 1976).
(Guide : Kumbhar). 1117

Public library legislation for Punjab : A draft—Manju Dua.
(Punjab University, 1981). 1118

Role of library legislation in the development of Public libraries with special reference to India—Habib-ur-Rehman Abdulkarim Khan.
(Bombay University, 1969). 1119

Public libraries—Maharashtra

Public libraries in Marathwada : A survey—A.A. Vaishwanar.
(SNDT Women's University, 1984). 1120

Entry No.

Public libraries—Movement

History and development of public library movement in Kerala during 20th century with special reference to Kottayam district : A survey—George Abe.
(Dharwar University, 1978).
(Guide : Kumbhar). 1121

Library movement in Assam from 1947-76—Meerabala.
(Punjab University, 1977). 1122

Library movement in Bengal—A.K. Datta.
(Punjab University, 1977). 1123

Public libraries—Pondicherry

Public library services in the Union Territory of Pondicherry : A survey—D. Anbu.
(University of Madras, 1982). 1124

Public libraries—Punjab

Municipal libraries in Punjab : A survey—Kuldip Singh.
(Punjab University, 1982). 1125

Public library development in Punjab : A development plan—Ameeta Ahuja.
(Punjab University, 1982). 1126

Survey of district libraries in Punjab—Daljit Singh Bhatia.
(Punjab University, 1977). 1127

Public libraries—Rajasthan

Public library services in Rajasthan—S.P. Sood.
(BHU, 1971). 1128

Public libraries—Tamilnadu

Connemara Public Library and District Central Library—Reading patterns—V.B. Govindakrishnan.
(University of Madras, 1980). 1129

Entry No.

Connemara public library : Its responses to social changes—R.K. Seethapathy.
(University of Madras, 1978). 1130

Mobile libraries in Tamilnadu with special reference to Madras—Samyukta Ravi.
(University of Madras, 1981). 1131

Public libraries in Salem district of Tamilnadu : A survey—M. Nallathambi.
(University of Madras, 1981). 1132

Public library system in Madras—
A. Thirumalaimuthuswamy.
(Dharwar University, 1974).
(Guide : Kumbhar). 1133

Tamilnadu public libraries : A case study—
B. Alagaperumal.
(University of Mysore, 1973).
(Guide : H.A. Khan). 1134

Tamilnadu public library service : A survey—
N. Avadaiappan.
(Kamaraj University, 1981).
(Guide : R. Paulmohan Roy). 1135

Public libraries—United Kingdom

Developing of public libraries in U.K.—Urmila Gupta.
(University of Rajasthan, 1978). 1136

Public libraries—United States of America

Public libraries in the United States of America—
M.S. Subramanian.
(BHU, 1970). 1137

Reference service

Current trends in reference service in India—
Anjali Kohli.
(Punjab University, 1984). 1138

Initiating college students to the use of library—
Mukesh Chawla.
(Punjab University, 1979) 1139

Entry No.

Place of reference service in Ranganathan's theory of library science—Piara Singh Dorka.
(Punjab University, 1984). 1140

Reference service in academic libraries with some case studies—Deepti Saxena.
(Vikram University, 1979).
(Guide : S. Kumar). 1141

Reference service : Its survey and programme in college libraries in Chandigarh—Joginder Pal.
(Punjab University, 1982). 1142

Reference sources

Research resources in the libraries of twin cities—Hyderabad and Secunderabad—Sreenivasa Sastry.
(BHU, 1981). 1143

Reference sources—Agriculture

Evaluation of Pusa Institute library with regard to Indian agricultural reference sources published during last ten years—Omprakash.
(University of Delhi, 1973).
(Guide : M.M. Kashyap). 1144

Study of development and growth of major research journals and reference sources in agricultural sciences—Satya Bhatia.
(University of Delhi, 1984).
(Guide : P.B. Mangla). 1145

Reference sources—British History

Study of literatures of British history during the medieval and modern periods from an American angle—P.K. Seal.
(Burdwan University, 1981). 1146

Reference sources—Buddhism

Evaluation of reference tools in Buddhism—Lodoe Sangpo.
(University of Delhi, 1984).
(Guide : P.B. Mangla). 1147

Entry No.

Reference sources—Engineering

Reference works in engineering—N.L. Trivedi (BHU, 1974). 1148

Reference sources—English

Evaluation of selected reference sources in physics, chemistry and biology in English language—Shailendra Kumar.
(University of Delhi, 1981).
(Guide : P.B. Mangla). 1149

Reference sources—Humanities

Major reference sources in humanities—Sarojini Negi.
(University of Delhi, 1982).
(Guide : C.P. Vasishth). 1150

Reference sources—India

Evaluation of collection of JNU library from the point of view of Indian reference sources—S.R. Gupta.
(University of Delhi, 1973).
(Guide : M.M. Kashyap). 1151

Evaluation of Indian reference sources in Delhi public library—A. Tripathy.
(University of Delhi, 1973).
(Guide : M.M. Kashyap). 1152

Evaluation of Indian reference sources published during last ten years available in Delhi university library—S. Gupta.
(University of Delhi, 1973).
(Guide : M.M. Kashyap). 1153

Evaluation of Indian reference tools available in the Jamia Millia Islamia university library—M.S. Usmani.
(University of Delhi, 1973).
(Guide : M.M. Kashyap). 1154

Entry No.

Evaluation of reference collection in central secretariat library—Amita Mehrotra.
(University of Delhi, 1983).
(Guide : J.L. Sardana). 1155

Reference works on India : A over-view of available material—N.N. Gidwani.
(Bombay University, 1968). 1156

Reference sources—Industry

Reference sources on industrial development (organised sector) in India : A bibliography—R.S. Singh.
(INSDOC, 1968).
(Guide : S. Parthasarathy). 1157

Reference sources—Law

Reference sources in law : An annotated bibliography—B.L. Ameta.
(Vikram University, 1983).
(Guide : G.D. Bhargava). 1158

Reference sources—Library Science

Characteristics of reference literature used by Indian library scientists—A.K. Kundu.
(BHU, 1982). 1159

Reference sources—Psychoanalysis

Reference literature on psychoanalysis in Punjab university : A survey—Ravinder Wahi.
(Punjab University, 1979). 1160

Reference sources—Science and technology

Indian reference materials on science and technology (1951-75) : A literature survey—R.K. Chibber.
(INSDOC, 1976).
(Guides : T.N. Rajan & K. Ramaswami). 1161

Scientific and technical resources in libraries in Marathwada region—S.D. Samangaonkar.
(SNDT Women's University, 1984). 1162

Entry No.

Reference sources—Vedas

Literature on and about the Vedas : A bibliographical survey—Dharmvir Singh Dahiya.
(University of Delhi, 1982).
(Guide : D.S. Aggarwal). 1163

Special libraries

AIR libraries in Karnataka : A study—C. U. Navalgund.
(Dharwar University, 1983).
(Guide : Kumbhar). 1164

Children's libraries : A study—M.V. Mudhol.
(Dharwar University, 1976).
(Guide : Kumbhar). 1165

Children's libraries in Karnataka State : A survey—S.P. Pavate.
(Dharwar University, 1981).
(Guide : Kumbhar). 1166

CIIL library : A study of resources in Telugu language and literature to teach non-Telugu people and to conduct research—T. Mercy Evangeline.
(University of Mysore, 1979).
(Guide : B. Nagappa). 1167

CIIL library : A study with reference to its resources—R. Rajalakshmi.
(University of Mysore, 1977).
(Guide : H.A. Khan). 1168

Concept of special libraries in India : Their development and role in the advancement of research and technology—M.S. Deogan.
(Punjab University, 1977). 1169

Conventional information services in special library—M.S. Srivastava.
(BHU, 1980). 1170

Development of libraries in Indian army—Basant Lal Yadav.
(Punjab University, 1979). 1171

Entry No.

Documentation services in special libraries of Hyderabad—M. Manikyarao.
(Osmania University, 1981). 1172

Ephemera and their treatment in special libraries—Nirmala Ruprail.
(INSDOC, 1966).
(Guide : K. Ramaswami). 1173

Library organisation of report literature in a special library—P.G. Joshi.
(INSDOC, 1966).
(Guide : T.S. Rajagopalan). 1174

Library services in special libraries of Hyderabad—N. Laxmanrao.
(BHU, 1971). 1175

Microforms in special libraries and their management—K. Dhawan.
(SNDT Women's University, 1984). 1176

Organisation of materials in linguistics and language teaching libraries—M.R. Riswadkar.
(Bombay University, 1972). 1177

Prison library system and reforms: A literature survey—Kanchan.
(University of Rajasthan, 1981). 1178

Role of ASLIB in the development of special librarianship—Gursharanjit Singh.
(Punjab University, 1978). 1179

Role of special libraries in advancement of research in India since independence—Jagdish Prasad.
(Punjab University, 1975). 1180

Special libraries and their problems with special reference to India—Omprakash Tiwari.
(Vikram University, 1974).
(Guide : A. Tejomurty). 1181

Special libraries in Himachal Pradesh : A study—Suresh Kumar Sharma.
(Punjab University, 1982). 1182

Special libraries in Karnataka : A study—B.V. Rajashekhar.

Entry No.

(Dharwar University, 1975).
(Guide : Kumbhar). 1183

Study of the resources and services of the Rotary children's library, Mysore—Mukunda.
(University of Mysore, 1983).
(Guide : H.A. Khan). 1184

Survey of periodicals acquisition and organisation in special libraries of Hyderabad—N. Satish.
(Osmania University, 1980). 1185

Survey of the library resources and services of selected Air Force library units in India with special reference to libraries situated in Bangalore—Sukhjit Kaur.
(University of Mysore, 1981).
(Guide : H.A. Khan). 1186

Use of books and other resources at SJCE library, Mysore—M. Puttannaiah.
(University of Mysore, 1981).
(Guide : H.A. Khan). 1187

Users Survey

College libraries of Ujjain city : A users survey—J.L. Garg.
(Vikram University, 1980).
(Guide : G.U. Bhargava). 1188

Constructive survey on the techniques employed in library user study programme—C.P. Ramesh.
(University of Mysore, 1978).
(Guide : P.K. Patil). 1189

Holkar Vigyan mahavidyalaya library, Indore and Motilal vigyan mahavidyalaya library, Bhopal : A users survey—Ramesh Pinge.
(Vikram University, 1979).
(Guide : G.D. Bhargava). 1190

Library services in Jabalpur university library : Users survey—P.C. Shrivastava.
(Vikram University, 1979).
(Guide : G.D. Bhargava). 1191

Entry No.

Public libraries in Delhi : A users survey—
Y.D. Chopra.
(Vikram University, 1978).
(Guide : G.D. Bhargava). 1192

Public library in Indore city : A users survey—
Surendra Singh Tomar.
(Vikram University, 1983).
(Guide : G.D. Bhargava). 1193

Readers' profiles and library use survey of college teachers teaching social sciences in the affiliated colleges of the university of Bombay—
M.G. Gowardhan.
(Bombay University, 1979). 1194

Readers' usage and interest survey of the university library, university of Bombay—S.A. Madiman.
(Bombay University, 1968). 1195

Readers' awareness about library services in Punjab university library, Chandigarh : A study—
Neeru Gupta.
(Punjab University, 1980). 1196

Readers' response to library services in Bangalore university libraries—K. Venugopal.
(Bangalore University, 1979). 1197

Services evaluation of Miranda House library from users' view point—Usha Gupta.
(University of Delhi, 1974).
(Guide : M.M. Kashyap). 1198

Socio-psychological study of library users of Bhagalpur university library : A survey work—
U.P. Yadav.
(Punjab University, 1977). 1199

Study of users' behaviour and needs at TIFR library, Bombay—S.S. Timble.
(SNDT Women's University, 1984). 1200

Survey of users' needs of library of university of Delhi—Yogendra Kumar Sharma.
(University of Delhi, 1972).
(Guide : B.V.R. Rao). 1201

Entry No.

Use of Hindi periodicals in central reference library of Delhi university library : A users' survey—Nirmal Diwan.
(University of Delhi, 1984).
(Guide : D.S. Aggarwal). 1202

Use of library by research scholars in Sri Venkateswara University : A study—M.R. Chandran.
(Dharwar University, 1976).
(Guide : Kumbhar). 1203

Use of scientific periodicals in selected subjects available in DULS : A users study—Shamsher S. Sahi.
(University of Delhi, 1983).
(Guide : J.L. Sardana). 1204

Users' survey of Andhra university English department library—G. Baburao.
(Andhra University, 1980).
(Guide : K. Sivareddy). 1205

Users' survey of Chowdhari Book Circulating library—D. Livingston.
(Andhra University, 1980).
(Guide : P. Somaraju). 1206

Users' needs study of Delhi School of Social work library—Yash Pal.
(University of Delhi, 1972).
(Guide : B.V.R. Rao). 1207

Users' preference of library : A case study of the British library, Hyderabad and City Central Library, Hyderabad—V. Vishwamohan.
(Osmania University, 1981). 1208

Users' survey concerning teachers and research scholars using Indian Institute of Technology, Delhi library—K.C. Sahoo.
(University of Delhi, 1978).
(Guide : Krishan Kumar). 1209

Users' survey concerning teachers and research scholars and students of Rattan Tata library—K.L. Dhall.
(University of Delhi, 1972).
(Guide : Krishan Kumar). 1210

Entry No.

Users survey of campus science teachers using the Delhi university library—C.V. Sasvanal.
(University of Delhi, 1972).
(Guide : B.V.R. Rao). 1211

Users survey of Delhi public library—Krishan Tiwari.
(University of Delhi, 1972).
(Guide : B.V.R. Rao). 1212

Users survey of Delhi public library, Karol bagh branch—Savitri Sharma.
(University of Delhi, 1973).
(Guide : M.M. Kashyap). 1213

Users survey of Delhi public library, Kasturba Gandhi Marg branch—H.H. Bharadwaj.
(University of Delhi, 1979).
(Guide : C.P. Vashisth). 1214

Users survey of Delhi public library, Laxmibai nagar branch—Anuradha Gupta.
(University of Delhi, 1973).
(Guide : M.M. Kashyap). 1215

Users survey of Delhi public library, Patel nagar branch—Vijaya Gupta.
(University of Delhi, 1973).
(Guide : M.M. Kashyap). 1216

Users survey of Delhi university library system regarding physics collection—Ravinder Pal Singh.
(University of Delhi, 1982).
(Guide : M.M. Kashyap). 1217

Users survey of department of Geophysics, Andhra university—K. Venkatareddy.
(Andhra University, 1980.)
(Guide : K. Sarada). 1218

Users study of departmental library : Department of Zoology, Delhi university—G.S. Achreja.
(University of Delhi, 1972).
(Guide : B.V.R. Rao). 1219

Users survey of Indian Institute of Public Administration—Shashiprapha.

Entry No.

(University of Delhi, 1980).
(Guide : C.P. Vashisth). 1220

Users survey of Institute of Economic Growth library —Unsart Bakht.
(University of Delhi, 1980).
(Guide : M.M. Kashyap). 1221

Users survey of Maulana Azad medical college library, New Delhi—K.C. Garg.
(University of Delhi, 1972).
(Guide : B.V.R. Rao.) 1222

Users survey of mobile library service of Delhi public library—Amalansu Sengupta.
(University of Delhi, 1973). 1223

Users survey of National Council of Applied Economic Research library —Bimla Kohli.
(University of Delhi, 1984).
(Guide : V.K. Sundaram). 1224

Users survey of National Medical Library—Ramprakash Dixit.
(University of Delhi, 1984).
(Guide : P.B. Mangla). 1225

Users survey of periodical literature in Indian Institute of Public Administration—S.K. Jain.
(University of Delhi, 1984).
(Guide : V.K. Sundaram). 1226

Users survey of reference collection in Indraprastha and Daulat Ram colleges—Sarita Gupta.
(University of Delhi, 1984).
(Guide : K.N. Gupta). 1227

Users survey of representative college libraries of tribal area of south east Madhya Pradesh—V.R. Chaudhury.
(Vikram University, 1982).
(Guide : S.S. Agrawal). 1228

Users survey of Shri Ram College of Commerce library—Veenarani Saini.
(University of Delhi, 1984).
(Guide : C.P. Vashisth). 1229

Entry No.

Users survey of south campus library (University of Delhi) Suman Bhatiani.
(University of Delhi, 1983).
(Guide : C.P. Vashisth). 1230

Users survey of students and teachers in social sciences of Indraprastha college and Laxmibai college —B.S. Panwar.
(University of Delhi, 1972).
(Guide : B.V.R. Rao). 1231

Users survey of the city central library, Dharwar—I.N. Kumbhar.
(Dharwar University, 1980).
(Guide : Kumbhar). 1232

Vikram university library, Ujjain : Users survey—Subhash Jain.
(Vikram University, 1981).
(Guide : A. Tejomurty). 1233

Women college libraries in Jammu : A users survey—Deshbandhu.
(Vikram University, 1979).
(Guide : G.D. Bhargava). 1234

LITERATURE

Assamese

Modern Assamese literature—S. Das.
(BHU, 1974). 1235

Literature—English

Bio-bibliography of a select Indian novelist writing in English—H. Sales-Pontes.
(Bombay University, 1978). 1236

English literacy criticism from Dryden to present day—M.L. Wali.
(BHU, 1966). 1237

English prose in Great Britain—M.V. Venugopal.
(BHU, 1966). 1238

Entry No.

Indian authors' contribution to English literature—Brij Bhushan Sharma.
(Punjab University, 1971). 1239

Literature—Hindi

Modern hindi criticism—K.K. Kamal.
(BHU, 1976). 1240

Sources of information in Hindi literature: An annotated bibliography—Kanta I. Puri.
(Punjab University, 1976). 1241

Literature—Kannada

Da. Ra. Bendre : Vyakti granthasuchi—M. Seetha.
(University of Mysore, 1982).
(Guide : Khaiser Jahan Begum). 1242

Women writers in Kannada : A biobibliography—A Janaki.
(University of Mysore, 1977). 1243

Literature—Malayalam

Women writers in malayalam literature : A biobibliography—V. Rajam.
(University of Mysore, 1980).
(Guide : R. Shalini). 1244

Literature—Tamil

Kavi Aracu Kannatacan : An annotated bibliography of his works and works on him—K. Nithyanandam.
(University of Madras, 1983). 1245

Literature—Urdu

Bibliography of Urdu poets—Khaiser Munnebulla Khan.
(University of Mysore, 1981).
(Guide : R. Shalini). 1246

MANAGEMENT SCIENCE

Evaluation of MBA and Diploma course level curricular and co-curricular book collection in the faculty of

Entry No.

management studies—R. P. Sharma.
(University of Delhi, 1982).
(Guide : Krishan Kumar). 1247

Management science—K. Pushpa.
(Andhra University, 1980).
(Guide : P. Somaraju). 1248

MATHEMATICS

Astronomy : Literature survey and trend during the 20th century—G. V.S.L. Narasimharaju.
(BHU, 1966). 1249

Bibliography of Indian statistical publications with subject index—Lola G. Nair.
(INSDOC, 1967).
(Guide : B. Guha). 1250

Mathematics and mathematicians in India during twentieth century—R.K. Nathwat.
(BHU, 1977). 1251

Origin, growth and development of mathematical journals : A pilot study—C. Arumugam.
(Kamaraj University, 1982).
(Guide : D.B. Krishnarao). 1252

MEDICINE

Abortion—Bibliography

Abortion, medical, legal and sociological aspects : A bibliographical study—M.L. Raina.
(INSDOC, 1970).
(Guides : S. Dutta and B. Guha). 1253

Antibiotics

Antibiotics literature survey and control—B.B. Bannur.
(Bombay University, 1974). 1254

Bibliography—India

Bibliographical control of medical literature in India—

Entry No.

Harvinder Kaur.
(Punjab University, 1974). 1255

Cancer

Recent advances in cancer research—Dura Raina.
(BHU, 1972). 1256

Cholera

Cholera literature survey and control—
M. N. Manohar.
(Bombay University, 1977). 1257

Cryosurgery

Cryosurgery : A trend report—P. Shankarlingam.
(University of Mysore, 1975).
(Guide : N.M. Pangannaya). 1258

Cytogenetics

Human cytogenetics—G. Padmavathi.
(Andhra University, 1980).
(Guide : P. Somaraju). 1259

Education

History of medical education (allopathy) in India :
Literature survey—G.C. Bharadwaj.
(University of Rajasthan, 1980). 1260

Erythroblastosis

Erythroblastosis : A trend report, 1972-77—
V. Venkataramana.
(University of Madras, 1979). 1261

Health hazards

Occupational health hazards due to exposure to chemicals : A trend report, 1974-76—
B. Gnana Sunder.
(University of Mysore, 1977).
(Guide : N.B. Pangannaya). 1262

Entry No.

History

Development of medical sciences from 18th century to the 20th century—Harjit Singh.
(Punjab University, 1983). 1263

Literature

Critical survey of the growth and development of literature in medicine in India since 1900 with special reference to the role of different institutions—B. Narayanarao.
(University of Delhi, 1968).
(Guide : V.K. Sundaram). 1264

Trend and bibliometric study of Indian medical literature—G. Philomina Mary.
(Kamaraj University, 1981).
(Guide : D.B. Krishnarao). 1265

Use of medical literature by gynaecologists : A case study—K. Srutakeerthi.
(Andhra University, 1981).
(Guide : B. Vijayalakshmi). 1266

Malaria

Eradication of malaria with emphasis to India—G.S.R. Varalakshmi.
(Andhra University, 1981).
(Guide : K. Sarada). 1267

Neuropathology

Decade (1966-75) on neuropathology in India : An analysis of citations—R. Pandurangarao Raju.
(INSDOC, 1976). 1268

Nursing

Nursing—Badriprasad.
(BHU, 1966). 1269

Nutrition

Nutrition during pregnancy : A trend report, 1978-81

Entry No.

—M.N. Malleswari.
(University of Madras, 1982). 1270

Nutrition of stressful environments : A report—W.P.E. Thomas.
(INSDOC, 1967).
(Guide : Dhanpat Rai). 1271

Periodicals

Ranking of periodicals in the field of medicine from the Indian scientists' point of view : A statistical analysis—Indra Narayan Sengupta.
(INSDOC, 1965).
(Guide : B. Guha). 1272

Psychopharmacology

Psychopharmacology—P. Vijaya Kumari.
(Andhra University, 1980).
(Guide : K. Sarada). 1273

Surgery

Plastic surgery—C.R. Karisiddappa.
(BHU, 1971). 1274

Recent advances in surgical sciences—G.P. Singh.
(BHU, 1971). 1275

Tuberculosis

Immunological survey of tuberculosis : A trend report—Vijaya Kumari.
(University of Mysore, 1978).
(Guide : T.V. Subramanyam). 1276

Vitamins

Food nutrition : Vitamins—M.K. Thulaja.
(BHU, 1972). 1277

Vitamin D : A trend report, 1974-75—M. Lakshmana Gowda.
(University of Mysore, 1977).
(Guide : T.V. Subramanyam). 1278

Entry No.

PHILOSOPHY

Ethical philosophy in modern European thought—G. Banurao.
(Andhra University, 1980).
(Guide : K. Sivareddy). 1279

Some metaphysical theories in western philosophy—Latarao.
(BHU, 1967). 1280

Vedanta philosophy—S.S. Koner.
(Burdwan University, 1980). 1281

Western philosophy—S.N. Khiste.
(BHU, 1968). 1282

PHYSICS

Advances in holographic inter-ferometry—P. Ratnakumar.
(Andhra University, 1980).
(Guide : B. Vijayalakshmi). 1283

Conferences on nuclear science and technology : A bibliographical study, 1967-69—Verghese Jacob.
(INSDOC, 1968).
(Guide : K. Ramaswami). 1284

C.V. Raman : A bio-bibliography—U.S. Deswal.
(INSDOC, 1971).
(Guide : R. Satyanarayana). 1285

Growth of periodical literature in physics during 1976-77—Sushma Dua.
(University of Delhi, 1981).
(Guide : J.L. Sardana). 1286

Laser—Bratati Neogi.
(Burdwan University, 1980). 1287

Laser : Research trends during 1958-62—Gulshan Mahajan.
(INSDOC, 1966).
(Guide : G.K. Arora). 1288

Entry No.

Laser technology—military applications : A trend report—Rajender Kumar.
(INSDOC, 1974).
(Guide : Dhanpat Rai). 1289

Solar energy—N.D. Livingston.
(Andhra University, 1980).
(Guide : P. Somaraju). 1290

Survey of electrode position of precious metals during 1969-73—K.V. Rangaswamy.
(INSDOC, 1974).
(Guide : N.V. Parthasarathy). 1291

Who is who and biography of the scientists working in the National Physical Laboratory, New Delhi—N.K. Wadwa.
(University of Rajasthan, 1981). 1292

X-ray methods in the study of defects in nearly perfect large single crystals—S.K. Phull.
(INSDOC, 1970).
(Guide : S.Z. Ali). 1293

POLITICAL SCIENCE

Bibliography

Bibliographical organisation and control on political science with special reference to India—T.K. Aduk.
(Burdwan University, 1981). 1294

Center-State relations

Centre-state relations in India—A.S. Chandel.
(BHU, 1974). 1295

Constitution—Fundamental rights

Constitutional amendments and fundamental rights—C.S. Champawat.
(University of Rajasthan, 1976). 1296

Constitution—India

Constitutional developments in India since

Entry No.

independence—R.K. Dave.
(BHU, 1970). 1297

Fundamental rights in Indian constitution—H.D. Mishra.
(BHU, 1973). 1298

Indian constitution—S.K. Srivastava.
(BHU, 1968). 1299

Defection

Defection in Indian politics : A literature survey—
C. Dekhan.
(Burdwan University, 1981). 1300

Democracy

Democracy—R.M. Khan.
(BHU, 1966). 1301

Role of Public libraries in a democratic set-up—
Nilima Datta.
(Burdwan University, 1981). 1302

Disarmament

Disarmament—Anirudh Prasad.
(BHU, 1968). 1303

Existentialism

Existentialism—Suchismita Sarkar.
(Burdwan University, 1980). 1304

Foreign Policy

Foreign Policy—Ved Prakash.
(BHU, 1966). 1305

Foreign Policy—India

Foreign policy in India—S.S. Janardanarao.
(Andhra University, 1980).
(Guide : G.V.S.L.N. Raju). 1306

India's foreign policy towards South-East Asia since
Independence—Chhabil Dass.
(BHU, 1974). 1307

Entry No.

Indo-Nepal relations, 1947-75—G.S. Limaye.
(BHU, 1976). 1308

Indo-Soviet relations under Nehru—Ramesh Kumar.
(BHU, 1973). 1309

Sino-Indian relations, 1947-65—S.S. Agrawal.
(BHU, 1972). 1310

Judiciary

Judiciary under Indian constitution—V.K. Srivastava.
(BHU, 1970). 1311

Literature

Structure of literature in political science—
S. Subramanian.
(Kamaraj University, 1982).
(Guide : A. Srimurugan). 1312

Local self-government

Local self-government—G.C. Srivastava.
(BHU, 1968). 1313

Periodicals

Growth of periodical literature in political science during the last ten years, 1968-77—Tejinder Kaur.
(University of Delhi, 1982).
(Guide : J.L. Sardana). 1314

Political movement

Andhra renaissance : A trend report on the social and political movement in A.P., 1900-1956—
P. Ramachandrarao.
(Andhra University, 1980).
(Guide : B. Vijayalakshmi). 1315

Political parties—India

Political parties in India—P.R. Purohit.
(University of Rajasthan, 1975). 1316

Entry No.

Study of a national political party of India : The Praja Socialist Party, 1947-67—J.S. Arora.
(BHU, 1970). 1317

Political systems

Indian political systems in national perspective—G.N. Mathur.
(BHU, 1976). 1318

Political systems in Sikkim since 1947—K.L. Awasthi.
(BHU, 1976). 1319

Public administration

Public administration—S.K. Khare.
(BHU, 1966). 1320

Sikkim

Transition of Sikkim—Shiela Ghatate.
(INSDOC, 1975).
(Guide : T.N. Rajan). 1321

Textbooks

Evaluation of textbook collection in political science for undergraduate and post-graduate courses in non-collegiate women's Education Board and School of correspondence course and Continuing Education library—Sarita Jain.
(University of Delhi, 1981).
(Guide : Krishan Kumar). 1322

UNO

UNO—K.G. Tyagi.
(BHU, 1967). 1323

Voting behaviour

Voting behaviour with special reference to India—P.K. Jayaswal.
(BHU, 1971). 1324

Entry No.

PSYCHOLOGY

Bibliometric analysis of the structure of the literature of social psychology—K. Sankaran. (University of Madras, 1980). 1325

Child psychology—Sulekha Roy. (Burdwan University, 1980). 1326

Educational psychology—P.N. Kaul. (BHU, 1967). 1327

Psychoanalysis—S.M. Tripathi. (BHU, 1966). 1328

Psychodiagnosis—Shobha Sharma. (BHU, 1967). 1329

Social psychology—Kanwaljit Singh. (BHU, 1967). 1330

Study of the obsolescene of periodical literature in the field of psychology—Joseph G.V. Vivekananda. (University of Mysore, 1978). (Guide : R. Shalini). 1331

Trends in developmental psychology—L. Ramaswami Sarma. (Andhra University, 1981). (Guide : B. Vijayalakshmi). 1332

RELIGION

Bhakti literature in Hindi during 15th and 16th centuries : A critical survey—Santosh M. Shola. (University of Delhi, 1968). (Guide : M.M. Kashyap). 1333

Buddhism in the east—P.L. Luchanarath. (BHU, 1972). 1334

Buddhism in the west—P.S. Kaeosri. (BHU, 1970). 1335

Hinduism and Buddhism : A comparative study—P.A. Namlao. (BHU, 1972). 1336

Entry No.

Literature on and about the Vedas : A bibliographical survey—Dharamvir Singh Dahiya.
(University of Delhi, 1982).
(Guide : D.S. Aggarwal). 1337

RESEARCH METHODOLOGY

Research methodology—Umesh Doanfal.
(University of Rajasthan, 1980). 1338

Research methodology of S. R. Ranganathan—Mohinderpratap Satija.
(Punjab University, 1980). 1339

Trend report on operational research—A.M. Arora.
(INSDOC, 1968).
(Guide : Dhanpat Rai). 1340

SCIENCE

Growth and development of selected reference tools in natural sciences published in India : A study—Girija Tickoo.
(University of Delhi, 1980).
(Guide : P.B. Mangla). 1341

Scattering of articles on tracer elements : A survey of scientific and technical periodicals—S.K. Jain.
(INSDOC, 1975).
(Guides : B. Guha and R.S. Yadav). 1342

Science periodicals in India : An appraisal—Hemalatha Balakrishnan.
(INSDOC, 1969).
(Guide : S. Dutta). 1343

RESEARCH

Development of scientific research in biological sciences in post-independence period in India : A survey—Harpal Kaur.
(Punjab University, 1976). 1344

Entry No.

Development of scientific research in physical sciences in post-independence period in India : A survey—Mohan Singh Pathania.
(Punjab University, 1976). 1345

Organisation of scientific research in India—Sawita.
(University of Delhi, 1983).
(Guide : D.S. Aggarwal). 1346

Scientific and technical research institutions in India—A directory : An outline of the organisation, development and observation—V. Sarangan.
(INSDOC, 1968).
(Guide : T.S. Rajagopalan). 1347

Societies—India

Scientific societies in India : A directory—A. Ratnakar.
(INSDOC, 1969).
(Guide : T.S. Rajagopalan). 1348

SOCIAL SCIENCES

Bibliography

Asian Social Science Bibliography : An operational manual—M.M. Sharma.
(University of Delhi, 1973).
(Guide : M.M. Kashyap). 1349

Bibliographical control in social sciences in India—Omkumari Chaudhary.
(University of Delhi, 1982).
(Guide : P.B. Mangla). 1350

Bibliographical organisation and control of social sciences—
(Burdwan University, 1981). 1351

Current bibliographical services in social sciences in India—Meena Nayyar.
(University of Delhi, 1984).
(Guide : V.K. Sundaram). 1352

Growth and development of bibliographical services in social sciences in India, U.K. during 1970s—G.W. Thakran.

Entry No.

(University of Delhi, 1980).
(Guide : D.S. Aggarwal). 1353

India

Survey of publications in social sciences published by the Union Government of India during 1966 and 1970—Jagdish Chander.
(Punjab University, 1973). 1354

ICSSR

Role of ICSSR for the advancement of research in social sciences—Neelam Rani Nakra.
(Punjab University, 1978). 1355

Periodicals

Manual of different set of operations involved in the preparation of Guide to Indian Periodical Literature : Social Sciences and Humanities—Satish Chander.
(University of Delhi, 1973).
(Guide : M.M. Kashyap). 1356

Social science periodicals in India : A study—Artikar.
(INSDOC, 1972).
(Guide : N.M. Ketkar). 1357

Union catalogue of social science periodicals in India : An experimental survey—S. Lakshminarayan.
(INSDOC, 1967).
(Guide : S.N. Dutta). 1358

Research

Alphabetico-subject index of Social Research, an international quarterly of Social Sciences, 1971-80—Alka Jain.
(Punjab University, 1983). 1359

Development of scientific research in social sciences in post-independence period in India : A survey—Ravinder Singh.
(Punjab University, 1976). 1360

Entry No.

SOCIOLOGY

Bibliography

Bibliographical services in sociology and anthropology in U.S.A. and India—S.P. Narang.
(University of Delhi, 1968).
(Guide : V.K. Sundaram). 1361

Caste system—India

Caste system in India—D. Janakidevi.
(Andhra University, 1980).
(Guide : P. Somaraju). 1362

Caste system in India—S.P. Sood.
(BHU, 1971). 1363

Census—India

Census of India : An inventory of source materials—J.L. Tekur.
(INSDOC, 1970)
(Guide : K. Ramaswami). 1364

Community development

Community development in India since independence—Lakshminarayan.
(BHU, 1970). 1365

Crime

Crime—G.S. Singh.
(BHU, 1968). 1366

Criminology—A. Meenakshi.
(Andhra University, 1981).
(Guidey : G.V.S.L.N. Raju). 1367

Criminology—S.K. Pandey.
(BHU, 1966). 1368

Customs—Kerala

Customs among Brahmins in Kerala : An analysis of change—C.V. Rajan Pillai.
(BHU, 1972). 1369

Entry No.

Family Planning

Family planning in India—R.N. Kaul.
(BHU, 1967). 1370

India

Recent trends in Indian sociology during last fifty years—Gurcharan Singh.
(Punjab University, 1982). 1371

Research work done in sociology in India between 1960 and 1970—L.N. Misra.
(Punjab University, 1973). 1372

Industrial sociology

Industrial sociology with special reference to India—A.K. Baradol.
(BHU, 1972). 1373

Juvenile delinquency

Juvenile delinquency : A trend report (1971-76)—P.R. Aruna.
(University of Mysore, 1977).
(Guide : H.A. Khan). 1374

Periodicals

Growth of periodical literature in the field of sociology in India during the last ten years—Sohan Lal.
(University of Delhi, 1979).
(Guide : D.S. Aggarwal). 1375

Journal literature of sociology : A bibliometric analysis—H.S. Geetha.
(University of Mysore, 1982).
(Guide : N.B. Pangannaya). 1376

Personality

Personality development—G. Misra.
(BHU, 1973). 1377

Entry No.

Political sociology

Political sociology : Scope and dispersal of documents —N. Anuradha.
(Bangalore University, 1977). 1378

Population

Demography—M. Rajbee.
(BHU, 1967). 1379

Demography : A citation study—C. Kalavati.
(University of Mysore, 1980).
(Guide : N.B. Pangannaya). 1380

Growth of India's population and the measures of its control—R.N. Pandey.
(BHU, 1973). 1381

Rural sociology

Rural sociology—Arbinda Chakraborty.
(BHU, 1967). 1382

Rural sociology—R.P. Rana.
(BHU, 1968). 1383

Rural sociological development in India—H.S.M. Amaruddin Ahmed.
(Andhra University, 1980).
(Guide : K. Sivareddy). 1384

Smoking

Smoking hazards : A trend report, 1976-78—S. Balasubramanian.
(University of Madras, 1980). 1385

Social welfare

Social welfare—N.M. Joshi.
(BHU, 1966). 1386

Society

Law and society—A. Mukhopadhyay.
(BHU, 1966). 1387

Entry No.

Tribal development

Role of public libraries in integrated tribal development—V. Chandrasekhararao.
(Andhra University, 1980).
(Guide : G.V.S.L.N. Raju). 1388

Tribal development in India—M. Satyanarayana.
(Andhra University, 1981).
(Guide : K. Sivareddy). 1389

Unemployment

Unemployment in India—A.K. Baradol.
(BHU, 1973). 1390

Unemployment problem in India—S.K. Samanta.
(Burdwan University, 1980). 1391

Urbanization

Urbanization in India : A study of problems and trends—P. Kumari Jyothsna.
(Andhra University, 1980).
(Guide : B. Vijayalakshmi). 1392

SPIRITUAL EXPERIENCE

Transcendental meditation—M. Krishnamurty.
(Andhra University, 1980).
(Guide : K. Sarada). 1393

STATISTICS

Critical survey of the growth and development of the literature containing Indian statistical data since 1900 with special reference to the role of different institutions like Central Statistical Organisation, New Delhi ; Indian Statistical Institute, Calcutta etc.—J.L. Sardana.
(University of Delhi, 1968).
(Guide : P.B. Mangla). 1394

Entry No.

TECHNOLOGY

Activated carbons : Manufacture and utilization : A trend report, 1966-69—M.M. Aggarwal.
(INSDOC, 1969).
(Guide : B. Guha). 1395

Analytical study of subject headings in the British Technology Index—B. Krishnamraju.
(INSDOC, 1972).
(Guide : B. Guha). 1396

Applications of plastics on defence : A trend report—R.N. Raghuraman.
(INSDOC, 1976).
(Guide : S.P. Pande). 1397

Biblioprofile on food science and technology with an indication of recent trends—G. Ramamani.
(Bangalore University, 1979). 1398

Biogas technology in India : A case study in information analysis and consolidation—A.P. Majumdar.
(SNDT Women's University, 1984). 1399

Energy sources for propulsion—B.K. Bharadwaj.
(INSDOC, 1973).
(Guide : M.L.N. Sastri). 1400

Journal literature of food science and technology : A bibliometric study—K. Suryarao.
(University of Mysore, 1982).
(Guide : B.S. Maheswarappa). 1401

Microthesaurus for documents on biopolymers—M. Narasimhalu.
(University of Madras, 1978). 1402

Modern weapons technology and effectiveness—M.N. Aggarwal.
(INSDOC, 1976).
(Guides : R.C. Garg and S.N. Ganguli). 1403

Single-cell protein from petroleum hydrocarbons : Trend report, 1961-70—B.R. Bhuyan.
(INSDOC, 1971).
(Guide : J.N. Baruah). 1404

Entry No.

Trend report on geranium oil—Hashmatara.
(Bangalore University, 1975). 1405

Vegetable edible oils : A trend report—
B.T. Kurahatti.
(Dharwar University, 1977).
(Guide : Kumbhar). 1406

UNIVERSE OF KNOWLEDGE

Universe of subjects with special reference to biological sciences—Madhu Kulsreshta.
(Vikram University, 1975).
(Guide : A. Tejomurty). 1407

USEFUL ARTS

Book trade

Book trade and academic libraries in Bombay city—
Tara M. Sheth.
(SNDT Women's University, 1981).
(Guide : Vidyut K. Khandwala). 1408

Printing—India

Early printing in Kerala : The contribution of the missionaries, 1577-1867—K.C. John.
(Bombay University, 1979). 1409

Evolution of printing by movable types in India : A study—Usha Bhatnagar.
(Punjab University, 1972). 1410

Publishing

Book publishing in India since independence—
Navjit Katyal.
(Punjab University, 1983). 1411

Publishing Prices

Average price index and publishing trends of Indian

Entry No.

publications in economics and statistics—S. Ansari.
(University of Delhi, 1969). 1412

Price and publication trends of books published in India during 1958-67—Mohindra Pratap Chand.
(University of Delhi, 1970).
(Guide : M.M. Kashyap). 1413

Price trends of Indian books in natural sciences, 1958 to Sept. 1967—N.S. Badhan.
(University of Delhi, 1970).
(Guide : M.M. Kashyap). 1414

Price trends of Indian books in physics, chemistry and geology—Premchand Kulleen.
(University of Delhi, 1970).
(Guide : M.M. Kashyap). 1415

Price trends of Indian books in sociology and education—Lalmaniprasad Singh.
(University of Delhi, 1969).
(Guide : M.M. Kashyap). 1416

Pnblication trends of Indian books in political science, 1958-66—H.D. Sharma.
(University of Delhi, 1969). 1417

Study of fluctuations in the prices of periodicals subscribed by Delhi University library in the field of chemistry and physics during the period 1970-1974—Rajeshwar Mishra.
(University of Delhi, 1976).
(Guide : Krishan Kumar). 1418

Reprography

Assessment of reprographic resources in agricultural university libraries in India—Jasbir Kaur.
(Punjab University, 1981). 1419

Document reproduction—R.P. Rana.
(BHU, 1968). 1420

Impact of electrophotography on document reproduction and documentation : A survey of the experience with the electrostatic process—J. Verghese.
(INSDOC, 1972). 1421

Entry No.

(Guides : K.S. Nagarajan and V. Ramachandran).

Recent developments in reprography : State of art report—N.S. Sreedhar.
(Bangalore University, 1977). 1422

Reprographic facilities in Madras city—C. Srinath.
(University of Madras, 1978). 1423

Reprographic services in Delhi—Bholaram Sachdeva.
(University of Delhi, 1975).
(Guide : M.M. Kashyap). 1424

Reprographic services in university libraries in India : A survey—Indubala.
(Punjab University, 1984). 1425

Reprography and its literature, 1961-66—B.R. Keshavarao.
(INSDOC, 1967).
(Guide : N.R.R. Chari). 1426

Reprography in India—R.K. Srivastava.
(INSDOC, 1979).
(Guide : P.V. Rao). 1427

Reprography in Punjab Agricultural University library, Ludhiana : A survey—Prithi Pal Singh Chopra.
(Punjab University, 1979). 1428

Reprography, methods and techniques—K.S. Chauhan.
(University of Rajasthan, 1977). 1429

ZOOLOGY

Growth of periodical literature in zoology during the last ten years, 1966-75—H.K. Yahya.
(University of Delhi, 1982).
(Guide : J.L. Sardana). 1430

Periodicals in the field of zoology in Delhi University library system—Narendra Kumar.
(University of Delhi, 1980).
(Guide : M.M. Kashyap). 1431

PART—II

NAME INDEX FOR MLIS DISSERTATIONS

Note : The number against each entry refers to the entry number of the items in Part I—Alphabetical Subject Part (MLIS Dissertations).

Entry No.

Entry No.

Entry No.

Entry No.

Entry No.

Entry No.

Entry No.

Entry No.

Entry No.

Chopra (R.N.).
Union catalogue of Library Science periodical holdings in DUL, JNUL and NSL, INSDOC. 322

Chopra (Veena).
Evaluation of selected reference tools in economics published in India. 292

Chopra (Y.L.).
Public libraries in Delhi : A users survey. 1192

Choudhury (B.K.).
Libraries of colleges affiliated to Utkal university : A survey and development plan. 422

Christie (E.R.J.).
Document acquisition policies and procurement with special reference to university libraries of Gujarat. 1053

Chugh (Kasturilal).
Evaluation of text book collection in history, political science, economics in B.A. (Pass and Honours) in select colleges. 380

Chugh (V.K.).
Bibliography of curricular and co-curricular level Hindi books in social sciences. 264

Cyril Royappa.
Study centres in Madurai-Kamaraj university area : A survey. 591

Dabas (R.S.).
Critical appraisal of the Hindu college library and Indraprastha college for women library buildings. 221

Dadarkar (P.R.).
Different classification systems used in pharmaceutical libraries in Bombay. 647

Dahal (Lella).
Survey of the National Medical Library with regard to its collections, services and uses. 453

Dahiya (Dharamvir Singh).
Literature on and about the Vedas : A bibliographical survey. 1163

Entry No.

Entry No.

Entry No.

Entry No.

Entry No.

Entry No.

Entry No.

Entry No.

Entry No.

Entry No.

Entry No.

Entry No.

Entry No.

Entry No.

Entry No.

Entry No.

Entry No.

Entry No.

Entry No.

Entry No.

Entry No.

Entry No.

Entry No.

Entry No.

Entry No.

Entry No.

Entry No.

Entry No.

Entry No.

Entry No.

Entry No.

Entry No.

Entry No.

Entry No.

Entry No.

Solomon (D.).
Higher secondary school libraries in Tirunelveli district : A survey. 474

Somnathan Nair (K.P.).
Study of the order supply correlations of books in the Kerala university library, Calicut university library, and Cochin univerversity library. 570

Somashekar. 467
Survey of school libraries in Mysore city.

Somashekar (K.T.).
Growth and development of agricultural education and libraries in India with special reference to Karnataka. 404

Sood (Asha).
Survey of libraries of India's missions abroad with special reference to UK, USA and USSR. 782

Sood (Neelam). 623
Contribution of Japan for automation in libraries.

Sood (S.P.). 1128
Public library services in Rajasthan.

Sood (S.P.). 1363
Caste system in India.

Sreedhar (N.S.).
Recent developments in reprography : State of art report. 1422

Sreedharappa (M.S.).
Evaluation of resources of Central Food Technological Research Institute Library, Mysore. 437

Sreenivasa Sastry. 136
Small scale industries in India.

Sreenivasa Sastry.
Research resources in the libraries of twin cities—Hyderabad and Secunderabad. 1143

Sreepathy Naidu (R.).
Scientific research and special libraries in India with special reference to Andhra Pradesh. 447

Entry No.

Entry No.

Entry No.

Entry No.

Entry No.

Vivekananda (Joseph G.V.).
Study of the obsolescence of periodical literature in the field of psychology. 1331

Vohra (P.N.).
Periodical literature : History and problems in library services. 338

Vohra (Ranjana).
History of library education in UK from 1900-1976. 856

Vyas (Lata).
Academic libraries in Gwalior city. 348

Vyas (P.K.).
Library buildings of Vikram and Indore Universities : A comparison. 225

Vyas (S.D.).
Acquisition section of the University of Delhi library. 530

Vythilingam (Rohini).
Comparative analysis of the abstracting and indexing periodicals in the filed of Laser Technology. 66

Wadhwa (N.K.).
Who is who and biography of the scientists working in the National Physical Laboratory, New Delhi. 1292

Wadikar (A.L.).
Development of academic libraries with special reference to University libraries in India. 549

Wahi (Ravinder).
Reference literature on psychoanalysis, in Punjab University : A survey. 1160

Wali (M.L.).
Research libraries. 445

Wali (M.L.).
English literary criticism from Dryden to present day. 1237

Walia (Harpreet).
Acquisition of periodicals : A case study of Punjab University library, PGI library and SCI. 576

Entry No.

PART III

INSTITUTIONWISE INDEX FOR MLIS DISSERTATIONS

Note :—1. Under each institution arrangement is chronological.

2. The number(s) against each year refer to the entry number(s) of the items in Part I—Alphabetical Subject Part (MLIS dissertations).

Andhra University (*Waltair*)

Year	Entry No(s)
1980	17, 20, 34, 143, 160, 166, 327, 331, 358, 360, 457, 476, 488, 489, 709, 734, 743, 750, 756, 906, 1046, 1205, 1206, 1218, 1248, 1259, 1273, 1279, 1283, 1290, 1306, 1315, 1362, 1384, 1388, 1392, 1393.
1981	2, 5, 14, 98, 103, 107, 142, 147, 174, 220, 359, 490, 707, 708, 755, 884, 915, 1017, 1040, 1084, 1266, 1267, 1332, 1367, 1389.

Banaras Hindu University (*Varanasi*)

Year	Entry No(s)
1966	106, 120, 149, 167, 626, 752, 795, 796, 797, 798, 800, 803, 805, 811, 813, 816, 820, 824, 825, 833, 1238, 1249, 1269, 1301, 1305, 1320, 1328, 1368, 1386, 1387.
1967	121, 155, 235, 315, 330, 344, 345, 357, 445, 455, 605, 686, 778, 877, 1004, 1051, 1060, 1080, 1094, 1115, 1237, 1240, 1280, 1323, 1327, 1329, 1330, 1370, 1379, 1382.
1968	8, 15, 62, 115, 118, 122, 127, 150, 227, 241, 435, 593, 594, 680, 692, 745, 746, 747, 759, 769, 804, 822, 823, 829, 844, 1081, 1170, 1282, 1299, 1303, 1313, 1366, 1383, 1420.
1970	18, 24, 63, 148, 154, 161, 236, 240, 644, 786, 814, 815, 835, 1059, 1074, 1137, 1297, 1311, 1317, 1335, 1365.
1971	3, 4, 42, 102, 124, 139, 173, 182, 189, 230, 260, 340, 354, 618, 912, 1007, 1008, 1045, 1085, 1128, 1175, 1274, 1275, 1324, 1363.

Year	Entry No(s)
1972	6, 23, 137, 153, 337, 341, 649, 669, 683, 799, 801, 806, 832, 1087, 1256, 1277, 1310, 1334, 1336, 1369, 1373.
1973	238, 776, 780, 781, 812, 819, 1298, 1309, 1377, 1381, 1390.
1974	12, 76, 171, 228, 834, 843, 1006, 1148, 1235, 1295, 1307.
1975	615, 996.
1976	136, 339, 583, 585, 612, 666, 710, 817, 818, 895, 898, 913, 1143, 1308, 1318, 1319.
1977	697, 1089, 1251.
1978	16, 35, 36, 38, 40, 181, 194, 491, 592, 595, 670, 886, 922.
1979	7, 77, 105, 112, 255, 439, 573, 639, 768, 809, 865, 866, 867, 900, 901, 910, 933, 959, 966.
1980	88.
1982	1159.
	Bangalore University (*Bangalore*)
1975	248, 872, 1405.
1976	123.
1977	691, 837. 861, 973, 1378, 1422.
1978	109, 205, 208, 407, 874.
1979	192, 486, 775, 894, 1197, 1398.
	INSDOC (*New Delhi*)
1965	83, 111, 214, 653, 716, 717, 758, 875, 975, 1272.
1966	10, 11, 13, 85, 90, 129, 203, 213, 271, 283, 761, 870, 876, 880, 1173, 1174, 1288.
1967	80, 84, 91, 95, 108, 199, 217, 275, 314, 631, 828, 952, 1250, 1271, 1358, 1426.
1968	19, 37, 131, 274, 882, 1157, 1284, 1340, 1347.
1969	81, 145, 146, 164, 332, 622, 718, 879, 931, 948, 1075, 1343, 1348, 1395.
1970	82, 132, 202, 211, 254, 328, 335, 770, 918, 923, 1253, 1293, 1364.
1971	79, 625, 851, 907, 919, 1072, 1285, 1404.
1972	58, 125, 216, 329, 333, 1357, 1396, 1421.
1973	9, 32, 97, 134, 152, 200, 234, 802, 1400.
1974	209, 645, 864, 868, 921, 943, 963, 1289, 1291.

Year	Entry No (s).
1975	28, 39, 78, 93, 96, 133, 207, 212, 218, 724, 1321, 1342.
1976	92, 99, 204, 215, 232, 748, 881, 1161, 1268, 1397, 1403.
1978	128, 130, 917, 924, 929, 937, 953, 967, 972, 979.
1979	126, 135, 138, 201, 1050, 1427.
	Karnataka University (Dharwar)
1972	400, 447, 472, 1105.
1973	433, 558.
1974	464, 784, 1133.
1975	405, 1106, 1183.
1976	575, 672, 849, 1052, 1086, 1093, 1108, 1117, 1165, 1203.
1977	187, 188, 442, 473, 485, 664, 902, 1104, 1406.
1978	363, 421, 456, 892, 920, 982, 1121.
1979	406, 422, 614, 711, 831.
1980	395, 430, 436, 643, 766, 1232.
1981	185, 401, 470, 557, 561, 1109, 1166.
1982	186, 463, 1066, 1102.
1983	399, 444, 465, 487, 563, 1065, 1103, 1164.
	Madurai-Kamaraj University (Madurai)
1980	279, 432, 474, 591.
1981	87, 245, 679, 714, 719, 1135, 1265.
1982	94, 590, 713, 1252, 1312.
	Osmania University (Hyderabad)
1980	659, 1185.
1981	1172, 1208.
1982	313, 364, 366.
	Punjab University (Chandigarh)
1971	119, 334, 480, 671, 725, 1024, 1028, 1048, 1099, 1239.
1972	278, 552, 690, 742, 757, 782, 846, 1010, 1410.
1973	184, 501, 502, 503, 600, 1030, 1031, 1095, 1354, 1372.
1974	423, 616, 668, 779, 908, 988, 1022, 1032, 1043, 1044, 1068, 1114, 1255.
1975	1, 45, 168, 318, 493, 496, 497, 855, 989, 997, 1033, 1180.
1976	336, 396, 494, 495, 498, 499, 551, 841, 1009, 1034, 1241, 1344, 1345, 1360.
1977	576, 577, 580, 623, 642, 665, 684, 773, 856, 857, 858,

Year	Entry No (s)
	990, 1018, 1019, 1020, 1021, 1023, 1029, 1041, 1122, 1123, 1127, 1169, 1199.
1978	249, 526, 527, 528, 553, 736, 737, 1016, 1025, 1071, 1179, 1355.
1979	46, 158, 253, 280, 397, 482, 570, 629, 738, 791, 998, 1013, 1078, 1139, 1160, 1171, 1428.
1980	170, 233, 247, 424, 446, 481, 675, 740, 741, 838, 850, 994, 1027, 1088, 1196, 1339.
1981	197, 276, 277, 300, 312, 343, 578, 608, 610, 648, 661, 739, 751, 760, 916, 956, 980, 1069, 1097, 1118, 1419.
1982	31, 459, 581, 808, 893, 899, 903, 958, 964, 987, 1011, 1116, 1125, 1126, 1142, 1182, 1371.
1983	47, 177, 349, 350, 458, 597, 598, 603, 621, 624, 633, 640, 660, 696, 790, 839, 925, 951, 999, 1037, 1054, 1096, 1263, 1359, 1411.
1984	33, 195, 196, 607, 613, 694, 845, 853, 854, 860, 862, 954, 976, 983, 992, 1015, 1063, 1067, 1138, 1140, 1425.
	SNDT Women's University (Bombay)
1980	272.
1981	206, 420, 568, 572, 620, 1058, 1408.
1982	871.
1983	647, 883, 890, 896, 946.
1984	1039, 1120, 1176, 1200, 1399.
	University of Bombay (Bombay).
1968	1156, 1195.
1969	550, 1119.
1970	191, 418.
1971	342, 656, 891, 993.
1972	237, 638, 1177.
1973	261, 783.
1974	469, 991, 1254.
1975	419, 646.
1976	637, 821, 911.
1977	175, 1012, 1257.
1978	1236.
1979	1194, 1409.
1980	441.

Year	Entry No(s)
1981	281.
	University of Burdwan (Burdwan).
1980	231, 346, 1281, 1287, 1304, 1326, 1391.
1981	104, 116, 1146, 1294, 1300, 1302, 1351.
	University of Delhi (Delhi).
1964	338, 678, 1049, 1082.
1968	89, 140, 169, 259, 270, 290, 291, 292, 294, 1264, 1333, 1361, 1394.
1969	387, 388, 658, 1412, 1416, 1417.
1970	262, 263, 264, 285, 286, 288, 535, 536, 537, 657, 1413, 1414, 1415.
1971	284, 287, 289, 293, 295, 297, 298, 461, 530, 542, 545.
1972	1090, 1201, 1207, 1210, 1211, 1212, 1219, 1222, 1231.
1973	61, 794, 1144, 1151, 1152, 1153, 1154, 1213, 1215, 1216, 1223, 1349, 1356.
1974	26, 52, 57, 73, 141, 221, 223, 224, 351, 389, 390, 448, 1005, 1198.
1975	273, 377, 381, 382, 383, 391, 506, 687, 688, 689, 762, 1424.
1976	50, 282, 317, 347, 372, 384, 393, 462, 601, 602, 604, 609, 827, 830, 836, 970, 981, 1418.
1977	162, 163, 256, 265, 316, 321, 452, 453, 512, 513, 514, 515, 516, 517, 518, 519, 520, 531, 673, 733, 789, 909.
1978	222, 257, 302, 303, 305, 307, 309, 368, 369, 370, 373, 374, 375, 386, 533, 540, 541, 652, 1091, 1209.
1979	70, 100, 101, 114, 319, 322, 376, 378, 392, 449, 544, 628, 842, 957, 1214, 1375.
1980	69, 72, 258, 301, 304, 306, 371, 532, 539, 636, 651, 1220, 1221, 1341, 1353, 1431.
1981	68, 71, 74, 113, 151, 159, 250, 308, 547, 721, 904, 941, 955, 1149, 1286, 1322.
1982	511, 641, 663, 685, 700, 701, 702, 703, 730, 749, 961, 1150, 1163, 1217, 1247, 1314, 1350, 1430.
1983	65, 299, 380, 385, 529, 538, 543, 611, 699, 704, 722, 726, 729, 731, 863, 1155, 1204, 1230, 1346.
1984	51, 266, 310, 394, 450, 451, 460, 546, 548, 632, 650, 706, 1062, 1145, 1147, 1202, 1224, 1225, 1226, 1227, 1229, 1352.

Year	Entry No(s)
	University of Kerala (Trivandrum).
1980	198, 296, 414, 509, 566, 599.
1981	567, 571, 792, 1055.
1982	44, 570, 667, 930, 974, 1056, 1110.
	University of Madras (Madras).
1978	268, 434, 627, 720, 950, 1130, 1402, 1423.
1979	112, 252, 413, 569, 1083, 1261.
1980	193, 949, 1036, 1129, 1325, 1385.
1981	183, 219, 431, 475, 588, 715, 889, 934, 944, 1070, 1131, 1132.
1982	362, 727, 873, 885, 928, 936, 960, 962, 1124, 1270.
1983	66, 67, 251, 361, 367, 728, 753, 878, 926, 927, 942, 1245.
	University of Mysore (Mysore).
1972	437, 507, 560, 1107.
1973	404, 443, 1101, 1134.
1974	267, 402, 589, 596.
1975	210, 408, 411, 523, 676, 1258.
1976	117, 438, 466, 522, 524, 525.
1977	229, 403, 409, 410, 492, 1057, 1168, 1243, 1262, 1278, 1374.
1978	41, 156, 556, 940, 1001, 1111, 1189, 1276, 1331.
1979	25, 27, 59, 165, 365, 564, 1167.
1980	22, 505, 508, 521, 735, 869, 1244, 1380.
1981	454, 559, 565, 662, 712, 1042, 1186, 1187, 1246.
1982	29, 144, 562, 695, 754, 777, 888, 1038, 1242, 1376, 1401.
1983	311, 412, 467, 555, 887, 939, 947, 1184.
	University of Poona (Poona).
1980	179, 471, 630.
1981	269, 500, 938.
1982	852, 905, 1076.
	University of Rajasthan (Jaipur).
1975	244, 674, 765, 826, 1316.
1976	785, 984, 1077, 1296.
1977	320, 477, 764, 774, 978, 1098, 1429.
1978	53, 64, 353, 428, 554, 606, 619, 682, 767, 847, 848, 1014,

Year	Entry No(s)
	1047, 1079, 1092, 1113, 1136.
1979	86, 190, 352, 355, 356, 398, 426, 478, 479, 534, 574, 579, 584, 587, 617, 677, 787, 793, 807, 932, 945, 968, 971, 1035.
1980	56, 157, 226, 429, 440, 484, 582, 681, 859, 935, 985, 1026, 1061, 1260, 1338.
1981	48, 49, 60, 176, 242, 243, 425, 427, 483, 586, 635, 977, 1178, 1292.
	Vikram University (Ujjain).
1973	21, 810.
1974	549, 840, 1100, 1181.
1975	723, 772, 1053, 1407.
1976	43, 246, 1000,
1977	771, 897, 1073.
1978	468, 732, 788, 1192.
1979	348, 763, 969, 1141, 1190, 1191, 1234.
1980	180, 225, 415, 417, 654, 1002, 1188.
1981	54, 75, 172, 416, 655, 698, 705, 744, 1064, 1233.
1982	239, 323, 325, 326, 693, 1228.
1983	30, 55, 110, 178, 324, 965, 995, 1003, 1158, 1193.

SECTION—B

DOCTORAL THESES

PART IV

ALPHABETICAL SUBJECT PART

(Ph D Theses)

Entry No.

ANTHROPOLOGY

Changing Potters of Central Karnataka—
A.K. Baradol.
(Karnataka University, 1981).
(Guide : K.G. Gurumurthy). 1432

HISTORY

Leftwing in India : M.N. Roy and India politics, 1920-1947—S.M. Ganguly.
(Rabindra Bharati, 1980).
(Guide : S.K. Sen). 1433

LIBRARY AND INFORMATION SCIENCE

Academic libraries

Critical Study of the organisation and utilization of libraries in higher educational institutions in Kerala—M. Bavakutty.
(Kerala University, 1984).
(Guide : K.A. Isaac). 1434

Automation

Problems and prospects of automation in Indian libraries and information centres—P.S.G. Kumar.
(Gulbarga University, 1985).
(Guide : Dr. S.R. Gunjal). 1435

Entry No.

Bibliography

Critical Study of the bibliographies and documentation lists of printed Hindi literature published during 1838 to 1978—Kumud Kumar Kamal.
(L.N. Mithila University, 1983).
(Guide : Srinarayan Singh). 1436

Mahatma Gandhi : A descriptive bibliography—Jagdish S. Sharma.
(Michigan University, USA, 1954.) 1437

Marathitheel Kosh vangmaya (=Reference literature in Marathi)—V.V. Kulkarni.
(Nagpur University, 1980).
(Guide : B.S. Pandit). 1438

Buildings

University Library buildings in India : A critical appraisal—Rajwant Singh.
(University of Rajasthan, 1983).
(Guide : S.N. Srivastava). 1439

Children's libraries

Evaluation of children's literature in Telugu and the development of children libraries in Andhra Pradesh—Velaga Venkatappaiah.
(Andhra University, 1981). 1440

Citation study

Citation analysis of doctoral dissertations in social sciences—S.L. Sangam.
(Gulbarga University, 1985).
(Guide : Dr. S.R. Gunjal). 1441

Growth of literature and citation pattern among the Indian journals in the field of Botany, 1950-1980—M. Mahapatra.
(University of Burdwan, 1984).
(Guide : B. Mukherjee). 1442

Entry No.

Classification

Analysis of the problems in the recognition of the manifestations in the fundamental categories in the inter-disciplinary subjects—M.A. Gopinath. (Karnataka University, 1983). (Guide : M.R. Kumbhar). 1443

Campatibility among medical classification of cardio-vascular diseases—Sistal Seetharama. (Karnataka University, 1984). (Guide : M.R. Kumbhar). 1444

Concept of analytico-synthetic sheme of classification with special reference to Ranganathan, Barbara Kyle, Farradane and Foskett : A study—Ranjana Vohra. (Punjab University, 1984). (Guide : Jagdish S. Sharma). 1445

Contribution of Rajasekhara to the development of subject classification—Tarun Kumar Mitra. (Calcutta University, 1982). 1446

Development of an unified scheme of common subdivisions in general classification systems—A.Y. Asundi. (Gulbarga University, 1983). (Guide : Dr. S.R. Gunjal). 1447

Development of terminology in the field of library classification with special reference to Indian school of thought : A case study in terminology and development—K.N. Prasad. (Karnataka University, 1983). (Guide : M.R. Kumbhar). 1448

Expansion and modification of Dewey Decimal Classification (Ed 18) for classifying Indological books with special reference to Indian philosophy and Indian religion—Suraj Kant Pandey Sharma. (Punjab University, 1977). (Guide : Jagdish S. Sharma). 1449

Facet analysis and depth classification of agriculture —D.B. Krishnarao.

Entry No.

(University of Delhi, 1957).
(Guide : S.R. Ranganathan). 1450

Use of library classification schemes in Indian libraries with special reference to Delhi—Pushpa Dhyani.
(University of Rajasthan, 1981).
(Guide : S.N. Srivastava). 1451

Co-operation

Library cooperation in India—Subash Chandra Verma.
(University of Rajasthan, 1980).
(Guide : S.N. Srivastava). 1452

Documentation

Documentation and information activities in Bangladesh--Sirajul Islam.
(Banares Hindu University, 1984).
(Guide : P.N. Kaula). 1453

Finances

University library finances in Madhya Pradesh—A. Tejomurty.
(Vikram University, 1982).
(Guide : G.M. Tapkir). 1454

History

History of libraries and librarianship in modern India since 1850—Jogesh Mishra.
(Ranchi University, 1973). 1455

History of libraries in ancient India down to 1200 AD—Saryugjee Sahai.
(Bhagalpur University, 1977). 1456

Libraries and librarianship of ancient and medieval India from earliest times to 1850 AD—Bimal Kumar Datta.
(Calcutta University, 1963).
(Guide : Nihar Ranjan Ray). 1457

Entry No.

Libraries in medieval India—Anirudh Prasad.
(Bhagalpur University, 1977). 1458

Philosophy and techniques of library historiography in Hindi—Shiv Kumar Sharma.
(Gurunanak Dev University, 1978).
(Guide : Ramesh Kuntal Megh). 1459

Indexing

General theory of subject indexing language—Ganesh Bhattacharya.
(Karnataka University, 1980).
(Guide : M.R. Kumbhar). 1460

Structure of indexing languages and retrieval effectiveness—Hemalata Iyer.
(Mysore University, 1984).
(Guide : P.K. Patil). 1461

Optimum algorithm in Subject indexing systems—Atef Kamat Awad.
(University of Delhi, 1984). 1462

Use of corporate entries for the literature in science and technology : A bibliometric investigation of OCLN database—U.K.Tikku.
(Pittsburgh University, 1981). 1463

Information services

Study of the information sources and services of agricultural extension officers with special reference to technology transfer in agriculture—D.B. Eswarareddy.
(Karnataka University, 1983).
(Guide : K.S. Deshpande). 1464

Technical innovations in horticultural sciences : Diffusion problems—M. Bankapur.
(Karnataka University, 1985).
(Guide : M.R. Kumbhar). 1465

Information system

Design and development of an information system

Entry No.

for small industry—T.A.V. Murthy.
(Karnataka University, 1983).
(Guide : K.S. Deshpande). 1466

Knowledge

Bibliometric analysis of the impact of the growth of biochemical knowledge on other biological and medical sciences—Indranarayan Sengupta.
(Karnataka University, 1984).
(Guide : R.S. Deshpande). 1467

Legislation

Effect of library legislation on public library development in Andhra Pradesh—G.V.S.L. Narasimha Raju.
(Andhra University, 1983).
(Guide : K. Ramakrishnarao). 1468

Library legislation in India—R.L. Mittal.
(Gauhati University, 1972). 1469

Library profession

Factors Related to job performance in library organisation—Bhooshanlal.
(IIT, Delhi, 1984). 1470

Librarianship as a profession : A study of socio-economic background and professional orientation of the librarians in Delhi—H.R. Chopra.
(Punjab University, 1985).
(Guides : A.K. Anand and S.L. Sharma). 1471

Library use

Study of the effect of library use on academic advancement of post-graduate stndents in the M.S. University of Baroda—G.R. Sudame.
(M.S. University of Baroda, 1972). 1472

Entry No.

Literature use

Use of social science literature in India—Shambhu Narayan Singh.
(Banares Hindu University, 1984).
(Guide : P.N. Kaula). 1473

Manuscripts

Buddhist Manuscripts in Thailand—P.L. Nuchanarth.
(Banares Hindu University, 1985).
(Guide : P.N. Kaula). 1474

Movement

History of the library movement in India, 1901-1947 —Pan Singh Adhikari.
(Allahabad University, 1966). 1475

History of the public library movement in Western Maharashtra, 1805-1921—Shantaram Gajanan Mahajan.
(University of Poona, 1979). 1476

Periodical literature

Origin and development of periodical literature in English in India upto 1947 : A survey—Ramesh Pal Arora.
(Punjab University, 1982).
(Guide : Jagdish S. Sharma). 1477

Preservation

Museum method and the process of cleaning and preservation/library preservation—Minendranath Basu.
(Calcutta University, 1950). 1478

Preservation of historical records in libraries—S.P. Mehta.
(Jiwaji University, 1984).
(Guide : D.B. Srivastava). 1479

Entry No.

Public libraries

Development plan for public library system in the Karnataka State—Somaraya Royappa Ijari. (Karnataka University, 1984). (Guide : M.R. Kumbhar). 1480

Public Library system for the Gujarat State : A development plan—P.F. Patel. (Gujarat University, 1978). (Guide : M.R. Kumbhar). 1481

Rural library services and community analysis : A study of an Andhra village—K. Sarada. (Andhra University, 1984). (Guide : K. Sivareddy). 1482

Rural Public library network in Punjab : A study, 1947-1980—Jagtar Singh. (Punjab University, 1985). (Guide : Jagdish S. Sharma). 1483

Reading interests

Enquiry Into reading interests of pupils of standard VIII to X—Renu Goswami. (M.S. University of Baroda, 1983). 1484

Investigation Into the reading interests and habits of the first year degree course of Marathi students studying in colleges affiliated to the University of Poona—A.R. Dunakhe. (University of Poona, 1978). 1485

Reading interests of childern in India—A.S. Chandel. (Lucknow University, 1984). (Guide : L.S. Chopra). 1486

Reference tools

Reference tools in Kannada published since 1800 AD : A technical study—C.R. Krisiddappa. (Gulbarga University, 1984). (Guide : Dr. S.R. Gunjal). 1487

Resource sharing

Computerized decision supporting system for the

Entry No.

management of resource sharing network—
Y.P. Dubey.
(University of Pittsburg (USA), 1984).
(Guide : Allen Kent). 1488

Scientific and technical libraries

Science communication : Problems and prospects with special reference to scientific and technical libraries—Inder Vir Malhan.
(Punjab University, 1985).
(Guide : V.A. Kamath). 1489

University libraries

Management and organisational pattern of university libraries in Madhya Pradesh—
Chandra Kant Sharma.
(Ravishankar University, 1977).
(Guide : Madhusudan Dubey). 1490

Manpower management in university libraries in India : A survey of job satisfaction—K. Navlani
(Karnataka Uuiversity, 1985).
(Guide : K.S. Deshpande). 1491

Motivational dynamics and work efficiency in the university libraries—Jugal Kishore.
(Punjab University, 1979).
(Guide : Jagdish S. Sharma). 1492

Professional manpower needs in university and college libraries of Delhi, Punjab and Madhya Pradesh ; and their implications on library science education—Shalini Rewadikar.
(University of Delhi, 1985).
(Guide : P.B. Mangla). 1493

Reader's use of the university libraries in the North-Eastern region with special reference to the universities of Assam and Meghalaya—Meerabala Baruah.
(Punjab University, 1984).
(Guide : Jagdish S. Sharma). 1494

Entry No.

Study of the organisation, working and utility of the agricultural university libraries in Northern India—Ramgopal Prasher.
(Punjab University, 1985).
(Guide : Jagdish S. Sharma). 1495

University libraries in Madhya Pradesh—Alla Tejomurty.
(University of Rajasthan, 1985).
(Guide : S.C. Verma). 1496

User's study

Socio-psychological study of library users—Upendra Prasad Yadav.
(Bhagalpur uuiversity). 1497

LITERATURE

English

Mulkraj Anand : A critical bibliography—Hilda/A. Sales-Pontes.
(University of Loughborough (UK), 1985).
(Guide : John Lucas). 1498

Hindi

Hindi Kosh Sahitya : Sameekshatmak adhyayan—N.R. Kalbhor.
(Agra University, 1981).
(Guide : Udai Shankar Shastri). 1499

Kannada

Late Uttangi Chennappa and his Works—S.P. Gunjal.
(Karnataka University, 1978). 1500

Sanskrit

Astadikpals in literature and art—R.P. Goswamy.
(Poona University, 1980).
(Guide : M.K. Dhavalikar). 1501

Entry No.

POLITICAL SCIENCE

Administrative innovations in Bihar during national emergency—A. Jha.
(L.N. Mithila University, 1981).
(Guide : S.K. Jha). 1502

SOCIOLOGY

Students' unrest in the universities of Bihar, 1967-1972—P.N. Gour.
(Bhagalpur University, 1978). 1503

PART V

NAME INDEX FOR PH. D. THESES

Note : The number against each entry refers to the entry number in Part 4—Alphabetical Subject Part (Ph. D. theses).

Entry No.

Entry No.

PART VI

INSTITUTIONWISE INDEX FOR PH. D. THESES

Note : The number(s) against each entry refer to the entry number in Part 4 — Alphabetical Subject Part (Ph. D. theses).

PART VII

GUIDEWISE INDEX FOR PH. D. THESES

Note : The number(s) against each entry refer to the entry number in Part 4—Alphabetical Subject Part (Ph. D. theses).

SECTION—C

M. PHIL. DISSERTATIONS

PART VIII

M. PHIL. DISSERTATIONS

Entry No.

Acquisition

Periodicals

Ashok Kumar

Indicators of the use of periodicals : Development of a cost-effective model of periodical acquisition in libraries.
(University of Delhi, 1981).
(Guides : Mrs. V.K. Sundaram and M.M. Kashyap). 1505

College libraries

Arora (Renu).

Study of the problems of reader delinquency in college libraries of University of Delhi.
(University of Delhi, 1980).
(Guide : Krishan Kumar). 1506

Information

Gathering

Dhakar (Vandana).

Comparative study of the information gathering habits of physicists in selected institutions of Delhi.
(University of Delhi, 1980).
(Guide : Krishan Kumar). 1507

Needs

Sood (Asha).

Study of information needs of economists and a

Entry No.

proposed plan for a National Information System for Economics.
(University of Delhi, 1981).
(Guide : P.B. Mangla). 1508

Systems

Saraf (Veena).
Global information systems and programmes : A study.
(University of Delhi, 1984).
(Guide : P.B. Mangla). 1509

Inter-library loans

Wig (Sukanya).
Inter-library loan services in selected libraries in Delhi : A comparative study and suggestion for evolving a policy for future.
(University of Delhi, 1982).
(Guides : D.S. Aggarwal and K.N. Gupta). 1510

Library education

Arneja (Baljit K.).
Design and development of a need-based curriculum for management education of Library and Information Science personnel.
(University of Delhi, 1981).
(Guide : M.M. Kashyap). 1511

Bodhibukkana (Dhida).
Library education in Thailand.
(University of Delhi, 1982).
(Guides : M.M. Kashyap and C.P. Vashishth). 1512

Personnel

Narang (S.P.).
Motivation of professional personnel in special libraries of Delhi towards continuing education : A study.
(University of Delhi, 1982).
(Guides : Krishan Kumar and J.L. Sardana). 1513

Entry No.

Pullareddy (V.).
A study of job statisfaction of professional staff working in university and college libraries of Delhi.
(University of Delhi, 1980).
(Guide : M.M. Kashyap). 1514

Ved Prakash.
Attitude of school principals towards librarians and library services.
(University of Delhi, 1983).
(Guide : P.B. Mangla). 1515

Staffing Pattern

Rita Kumar.
Staffing pattern in selected types of libraries in Delhi.
(University of Delhi, 1983).
(Guide : D.S. Aggarwal). 1516

Thesaurus

Chandrashekhararao (Valavala).
Thesaurus of cell biology.
(University of Delhi, 1982).
(Guide : Krishan Kumar). 1517

SECTION—D

DOCTORAL RESEARCH IN PROGRESS

PART IX

DOCTORAL RESEARCH IN PROGRESS

Entry No.

Abraham (M.A.).
Designing of an information storage and retrieval system with special reference to satellite launch vehicle projects.
(University of Kerala).
(Guides : K.A. Isaac and G.S. Sukumaran). 1517A

Batra (Rashmi).
Library science education in India : A comparative study in India since 1947.
(Punjab University).
(Guide : U.K. Tikku). 1518

Bhan (Namita).
Evaluation and structure of library and information science education in India.
(University of Lucknow).
(Guide : P.N. Kaula). 1519

Champawat (G.S.).
Prison libraries : Their role in the reformation and rehabilitation of the inmates with special reference to India.
(University of Rajasthan).
(Guide : S.N. Srivastava). 1520

Devaranjan (G.).
An investigation into financing of Kerala, Cochin and Calicut University Libraries during the third, fourth and fifth plan period.
(University of Kerala).
(Guide : K.A. Isaac). 1521

Gandhi (T.M.K.).
Industrial libraries in Visakhapatnam : A case

Entry No.

study.
(Andhra University).
(Guide : K. Sivareddy). 1522

Ganpule (S.R.).
Models for measuring effectiveness of library services.
(University of Poona).
(Guide : M.R. Riswadkar). 1523

Garg (B.S.).
Job statisfaction among library personnel of State Universities of Rajasthan and University of Delhi.
(University of Rajasthan).
(Guide : Krishan Kumar). 1524

Gera (S.C.).
Scientific and technical libraries in India and information network.
(University of Rajasthan).
(Guide : S.C. Verma). 1525

Gopinath an Nair (N.).
A comparative study of the Colon Classification, Dewey Decimal Classification with special reference to their application to medical sciences.
(University of Kerala).
(Guide : K.A. Isaac). 1526

Gupta (Awadh Bihari).
Information services in medical libraries of India.
(Banares Hindu University).
(Guide : J.B. Subramaniam). 1527

Gupta (Sri Ram).
Maintenance and evaluation of information sources in professional college libraries of India : A study through the technique of system analysis.
(Banares Hindu University).
(Guide : P.N. Kaula). 1528

Hukmani (Padma).
Acquisition of serial publications in university libraries : System approach.

Entry No.

(University of Rajasthan).
(Guide : S.C. Verma). 1529

Indira (S.).
Collection, organisation and dissemination of economics literature in the university libraries in Andhra Pradesh : An analysis.
(Andhra University).
(Guide : K. Sivareddy). 1530

Johnson (E.).
Design and development of a national information system for marine fisheries in India.
(University of Kerala).
(Guide : K.A. Isaac). 1531

Kamaiah (Peripudi).
Personnel problems in library management of the university libraries in Andhra Pradesh : A study.
(Karnataka University).
(Guide : M.R. Kumbhar). 1532

Kapadia (Nirmala S.).
Computerisation of library services in India.
(University of Poona).
(Guide : M.R. Riswadkar). 1533

Kaushik (Purnima).
Universe of subjects and development in classification schemes with special reference to natural sciences.
(University of Rajasthan).
(Guide : P. Dhyani). 1534

Khanna (Brij Mohan).
Meteorological data services in India : Origin, development and current status.
(University of Poona).
(Guide : M.R. Riswadkar). 1535

Konnur (M.B.).
Indo-American cooperation in the field of library and information science.
(University of Poona).
(Guide : M.R. Riswadkar). 1536

Entry No.

Koteshwara Rao (S.).
Library facilities in post-graduate, under-graduate and junior colleges in Guntur, Krishna and Prakasham districts of Andhra Pradesh.
(Andhra University).
(Guide : K. Sivareddy). 1537

Majumdar (Kirit J.).
Management of serials in university libraries in India.
(University of Poona).
(Guide : M.R. Riswadkar). 1538

Malhotra (Harpal Kaur).
Use of Punjab Agricultural University Library and Haryana Agricultural University Library by post-graduate students : A comparative study.
(Punjab University).
(Guide : U.K. Tikku). 1539

Mishra (Dayashankar).
Development of notation for library classification : A comparative and critical study of classification schemes.
(Banares Hindu University).
(Guide : S.N. Singh). 1540

Mishra (Virendra Kumar).
Cataloguing of shared authorship : A comparative and critical account of the catalogue codes.
(Banares Hindu University).
(Guide : S.N. Singh). 1541

Narayana (G.J.).
Information as a commodity.
(University of Poona).
(Guide : M.R. Riswadkar). 1542

Natu (S.R.).
Development of public libraries in Maharashtra from 1967.
(University of Poona).
(Guide : S. G. Mahajan). 1543

Entry No.

Ojha (D.C.).
Role of libraries and information centres in technology transfer in arid and semi-arid areas.
(University of Rajasthan).
(Guide : C.D. Sharma). 1544

Pal (Satnam Singh).
Development of a model for University archives in India.
(Punjab University).
(Guide : Jagdish S. Sharma). 1545

Paras Nath.
Indexing systems and their application to information needs.
(Banares Hindu University).
(Guide : S.N. Singh). 1546

Pillai (P. Balakrishna).
Medical documentation in India and its impact on medical research.
(University of Kerala).
(Guide : K.A. Isaac). 1547

Prasad (H.N.).
Universe of subjects : Their fragmentation and association.
(Banares Hindu University).
(Guide : S.N. Singh). 1548

Ramjee Singh.
Pattern of literature used by researchers in the field of social sciences.
(Banares Hindu University).
(Guide : S.N. Singh). 1549

Satyanarayana (N.R.).
Problems of constructing bibliography for higher research in English literature.
(Lucknow University). 1550

Saxena (Amar Jyoti).
Resource sharing and NATIS in medical libraries.
(University of Rajasthan).
(Guide : S.N. Srivastava). 1551

Entry No.

Varma (Ajay Kumar).
Evaluation of reference sources in Hindi.
(Jiwaji University).
(Guide : S.M. Tripathi). 1552

Sharma (C.L.).
Bibliotherapy with special reference to India.
(University of Rajasthan).
(Guide : S.N. Srivastava). 1553

Sharma (C.R.).
A study of archives and libraries in Jammu and Kashmir.
(Punjab University).
(Guide : Jagdish S. Sharma). 1554

Sharma (Mridula).
Development of social sciences and problems in classification.
(University of Rajasthan).
(Guide : S.N. Srivastava). 1555

Sharma (Omprakash).
Library service to physically handicapped persons in India after 1947 : A study.
(Punjab University).
(Guide : Jagdish S. Sharma). 1556

Sharma (Sandhya).
Structure and development of public libraries in Rajasthan.
(University of Rajasthan).
(Guide : P. Dhyani). 1557

Somasekhara Rao (K.).
Junior college libraries in Andhra Pradesh.
(Andhra University).
(Guide : K. Sivareddy). 1558

Sood (S.P.).
University libraries in Rajasthan : Their development and management.
(University of Rajasthan).
(Guide : S.N. Srivastava). 1559

SECTION—E

LATER ADDITIONS

ANDHRA UNIVERSITY, MLIS DISSERTATIONS

1981-82

During 1981-82 MLIS course was not offered

1982—83

Entry No.

Bhadrakshi (V.).
A case study of R & D Laboratory Library : NSTL, Visakhapatnam.
(Guide : K. Sarada). 1615

Bhadrakshi (V.).
Land development banks in India.
(Guide : K. Sarada). 1616

Bhaskara Rao (P.)
Mass media and communication.
(Guide : G.V.S.L. Narasimha Raju). 1617

Bhaskara Rao (P.).
The UGC study centre : Nature and performance : A case study of Andhra University Centre.
(Guide : G.V.S.L. Narasimha Raju). 1618

Jaya Bheem (D.).
College libraries in Kakinada : A study.
(Guide : K. Siva Reddy). 1619

Jaya Bheem (D).
Sociology and family.
(Guide : K. Siva Reddy). 1620

Khan (Md.).
The status of women in the present society.
(Guide : G.V.S.L. Narasimha Raju). 1621

Khan (Md.).
Users' library survey of the department of psychology and parapsychology.
(Guide : G.V.S.L. Narasimha Raju). 1622

Entry No.

Krishna Kumari (K.).
Children library : A case study of children's branch library, Visakhapatnam.
(Guide : K. Sarada). 1623

Krishna Kumari (K.).
Civil services.
(Guide : K. Sarada). 1624

Narasimha Raju (A,P.S.V.V.S.N.L.).
Human blood groups.
(Guide : G.V.S.L. Narasimha Raju). 1625

Narasimha Raju (A.P.S.V.V.S.N.L.).
A survey of college libraries in West Godavari District.
(Guide : G.V.S.L. Narasimha Raju). 1626

Satyam Babu (N.).
Degree college libraries in Khamman District.
(Guide : P. Soma Raju). 1627

Satyam Babu (N.).
Pisces (Fishes) resperception and effects of various factors.
(Guide : P. Soma Raju). 1628

Sreeranga Venkateswara Rao (G.).
Kakinada Engineering College Library : A case study.
(Guide : K. Siva Reddy). 1629

Sreeranga Venkateswara Rao (G.).
Community development programme in India.
(Guide : K. Siva Reddy). 1630

Sugunamma (G.).
Computer performance evaluation.
(Guide : P. Soma Raju). 1631

Sugunamma (G.).
Computerized information system.
(Guide : P. Soma Raju). 1632

Veerabhadra Rao (R.).
Users' survey of Zoology Department.
(Guide : B. Vijayalakshmi). 1633

Entry No.

Veerabhadra Rao (R.).
Information retrieval system.
(Guide : B. Vijayalakshmi). 1634

Venkata Harikrishna Rao (G.).
Experimental psychology (human), 1978-1982.
(Guide : K. Sarada). 1635

Venkata Harikrishna Rao (G.).
Government Degree College Library, Srikakulam.
(Guide : K. Sarada). 1636

1983-84

Bhanoji (N.).
A. J. Kalasala Degree College Library, Machilipatnam.
(Guide : K. Sarada). 1637

Bhanoji (N.).
Rural sociology.
(Guide : K. Sarada). 1638

Hanumayamma (T.).
Agricultural production in India.
(Guide : B. Vijayalakshmi). 1639

Hanumayamma (T.).
Information use : A survey of the staff and researchers of the Department of Cooperation and Applied Economics, Andhra University.
(Guide : B. Vijayalakshmi). 1640

Prasad (P.).
Study of college libraries in Guntur.
(Guide : K. Sarada). 1641

Prasad (P.).
Animal paleontology.
(Guide : K. Sarada). 1642

Rama Devi (B.).
Trends in noise pollution.
(Guide : B. Vijayalakshmi). 1643

Rama Devi (B.).
A survey of information needs of engineers attached to defence organizations—NSTL NAD

Entry No.

and CIEFS.
(Guide : B. Vijayalakshmi). 1644

Ravibabu (P.).
Information use : A survey of the staff and researchers of the Department of Commerce and Management Studies, Andhra University.
(Guide : P. Soma Raju). 1645

Ravibabu (P.).
Labour wages in India.
(Guide : P. Soma Raju). 1646

Ravindranath (A.)
Ultrasonic studies in liquid crystals and liquid crystalline mixtures.
(Guide : K. Sarada). 1647

Ravindranath (A).
Radio engineering : A bibliometric study.
(Guide : K. Sarada). 1648

Satyanarayana (N.).
Citation analysis in literature of Information Science : A case study.
(Guide : K. Siva Reddy). 1649

Satyanarayana (N.).
Trends in adult education in India.
(Guide : K. Siva Reddy). 1650

Usha Bala (K.).
Banks and banking services in India.
(Guide : P. Soma Raju). 1651

Usha Bala (K.).
College libraries : A case study of S.K.B.R. College Library, Amalapuram.
(Guide : P. Soma Raju). 1652

Venkat Rao (P).
Central Institute of English and Foreign Languages Library, Hyderabad : A case study.
(Guide : B. Vijayalakshmi). 1653

Venkat Rao (P.).
Coastal aquaculture (Penaeid Prawn Culture).
(Guide : B. Vijayalakshmi). 1654

Entry No.

Kanakachary (M.).
A case study of Kakatiya University Library, Warangal.
(Guide : B. Vijayalakshmi). 1655

Murali Kishore (N.).
Seismology.
(Guide : K. Siva Reddy). 1656

Nageswara Rao (G.).
The Nagarjuna University Library : A survey.
(Guide : B. Vijayalakshmi). 1657

Sivarama Prasad (M.).
Reclamation of Alkali Soils in India.
(Guide : P. Soma Raju). 1658

Srilakshmi Sujatha (K.).
A study of State Regional Library, Guntur..
(Guide : K. Sarada). 1659

Tatarao (K.).
Postgraduate Centre Library, Anakapalle : A case study.
(Guide : P. Soma Raju). 1660

Valasayya (G.).
Indian horticulture—Mango.
(Guide : K. Siva Reddy). 1661

Vijaya Kumari (M.).
Social Science Research on mangement of major irrigation projects in India.
(Guide : K. Sarada). 1662

Vijayalakshmi (D.V.).
Trends on Open University Library System.
(Guide : P. Soma Raju). 1663

Vijayalaksmi (P.).
St. Joseph's College Library : A study.
(Guide : K. Sarada). 1664

NAGPUR UNIVERSITY, MLIS DISSERTATIONS
1984-85

Entry No.

Baheti (S.R.).
Status and service conditions of college librarians in Vidarbha region.
(Guide : P.S.G. Kumar). 1665

Bhosle (Balaji K.).
Study of use of catalogues in Nagpur university library.
(Guide : N.H. Pawar). 1666

Deshpande (S.W.).
Evaluation of the role of Government Divisional Library, Nagpur in the development of public libraries in Vidarbha region.
(Guide : S. K. Kesarwani). 1667

Dhavle (V.N.).
College libraries in Nagpur city.
(Guide : V.V. Kulkarni). 1668

Gajway (P.M).
Literature survey and trends in library cataloguing, 1970-1975.
(Guide : N.H. Pawar). 1669

Jatkar (R.B.).
Periodicals resource sharing among college libraries of Amravati : A blue print.
(Guide : S.K. Kesarwani). 1670

Kale (V.E.).
Reprographic facilities available in the city of Nagpur.
(Guide : S.G. Bhat). 1671

Ladsaongikar (P.K.).
Citation analysis of M.Tech (IPS) dissertations submitted to the Nagpur University.
(Guide : S.G. Bhat). 1672

Entry No.

Memavarkar (U.G.).
National Information Centre for Library and Information Science (NICLIS) : A plan.
(Guide : P.S.G. Kumar). 1673

Rajyalakshmi (D.).
Literature survey and trends in cataloguing, 1960-1969.
(Guide : P.S.G. Kumar). 1674

Vinchurkar (A.W.).
Literature survey and trends in library cataloguing, 1950-1959.
(Guide : P.S.G. Kumar). 1975

OSMANIA UNIVERSITY, MLIS DISSERTATIONS 1978-1979

Entry No.

Gangadhar (S.).
Reading habits of rural community of Nizamabad : A case study.
(Guide : N. Laxman Rao). 1676

Gangadhar (S.).
Rural development in India : Bibliographical sources and services.
(Guide : A.A.N. Raju). 1677

Jaggarao (N.V.).
Lexicons and lexicographical writing in Telugu.
(Guide : M.V. Venugopal). 1678

Jaggarao (N.V.).
Staff pattern in university libraries in Andhra Pradesh : A comparative study.
(Guide : B.P. Shenoy). 1679

Laxminarayana (G.).
Procurement of Government of India publications.
(Guide : A.A.N. Raju). 1680

Laxminarayana (G.).
Industrial financing in India : An overview of literature.
(Guide : R.K. Gupta). 1681

Sateesh (N.).
Survey of library resources and information services in agricultural libraries of Andhra Pradesh.
(Guide : B.P. Shenoy). 1682

Sateesh (N.).
Survey of periodical acquisition and organisation in special libraries of Hyderabad.
(Guide : A.A.N. Raju). 1683

Entry No.

Shafeeuddin.
Theses and dissertations collection in Iraq : A critical appraisal of the problem of organisation and control.
(Guide : M.V. Venugopal). 1684

Shafeeuddin.
English language teaching : A study of information sources in India.
(Guide : M.V. Venugopal). 1685

Sudershan Rao (S.).
Urban planning and development in India : A brief survey of institutions/agencies and sources of information.
(Guide : B.P. Shenoy). 1686

Sudershan Rao (S.).
Information requirements of researchers : A user survey of special libraries in twin cities of Hyderabad and Secunderabad.
(Guide : N. Laxman Rao). 1687

Takalkar (Anil).
Critical evaluation of reader services in special libraries in twin cities.
(Guide : R.K. Gupta). 1688

Takalkar (Anil).
Rural development information system : A national plan.
(Guide : R.K. Gupta). 1689

Yadagiri Reddy (J.).
Telugu novel (1960-1965) : A bibliography and review.
(Guide : M.V. Venugopal). 1690

Yadagiri Reddy (J.).
Cataloguing operations in major libraries of twin cities of Hyderabad and Secunderabad.
(Guide : B.P. Shenoy). 1691

Entry No.

1980-1981

Inamdar (Anagha).
A study of the working of campus and constituent college libraries of Osmania University.
(Guide : A.A.N. Raju). 1692

Inamdar (Anagha).
Panchayatiraj in Andhra Pradesh : A literature survey.
(Guide : N. Laxman Rao). 1693

Manikya Rao (M.).
Small scale industries in Andhra Pradesh, 1971-1981.
(Guide : R.K. Gupta). 1694

Manikya Rao (M.).
Documentation service in special libraries of Hyderabad.
(Guide : N. Laxman Rao). 1695

Prafulla Chandra.
A study of the professional staff in the public libraries of Hyderabad.
(Guide : R.K. Gupta). 1696

Prafulla Chandra.
Land reforms in Andhra Pradesh since 1956.
(Guide : B.P. Shenoy). 1697

Urmila Reddy.
Development of higher education in India since Kothari Commission (1964-1966).
(Guide : R.K. Gupta). 1698

Urmila Reddy.
Readers' services in special libraries of Hyderabad.
(Guide : B.P. Shenoy). 1699

Vishwa Mohan.
Users' preference of library : A case study of British Library, Hyderabad and City Central Library, Hyderabad.
(Guide ; M.V Venugopal). 1700

Entry No.

Vishwa Mohan.
Andhra Pradesh archaeology from 1956 : A literature survey and trend report.
(Guide : A.A.N. Raju). 1701

1981-1982

Durvasa Babu (A.).
Book selection in major university libraries in Andhra Pradesh.
(Guide : B.P. Shenoy). 1702

Durvasa Babu (A.).
Local history of Alampur.
(Guide : M.V. Venugopal). 1703

Jacob (Gnan Sunder).
A brief history and critical appraisal of development of study and research in earth sciences in India.
(Guide : M.V. Venugopal). 1704

Jacob (Gnan Sunder).
The journal literature of earth science : A study based on Indian Science Abstracts, 1980.
(Guide : A.A.N. Raju). 1705

Kulkarni (N.D.).
Comparative study of existing public library acts in India.
(Guide : N. Laxman Rao). 1706

Kulkarni (N.D.).
Adult education in Andhra Pradesh.
(Guide : A.A.N. Raju). 1707

Ramakrishna (D.).
Use of audio-visual aids in class room teaching : A literature survey and trend report.
(Guide : R.K. Gupta). 1708

Ramakrishna (D.).
Library extension activity : A study.
(Guide : B.P. Shenoy). 1709

Seetha.
Library science literature published in Indian

Entry No.

periodicals : An analysis.
(Guide : A.A.N. Raju). 1710

Seetha.
Irrigation projects in Andhra Pradesh from 1956-1980.
(Guide : B.P. Shenoy). 1711

Shamala (A.).
Readers' services in the defence libraries of twin cities : A survey.
(Guide : N. Laxman Rao). 1712

Shamala (A.).
Leadership in the army.
(Guide : R.K. Gupta). 1713

Sudhakar Goud (K.).
Indian foreign policy, 1977-1980 : A trend report.
(Guide : B.P. Shenoy). 1714

Sudhakar Goud (K.).
Resource sharing of periodicals in chemistry and allied sciences in the Osmania University Campus area : A case study.
(Guide : R.K. Guptal). 1715

1982-83

Chandran (D.).
Management of engineering college libraries in Telengana areas : A survey.
(Guide : N. Laxman Rao). 1716

Chandrashekar reddy (R.).
Users' survey of research scholars : Department of Chemistry, Osmania University.
(Guide : A.A.N. Raju). 1717

Deshpande (Suneeti).
A comparative study of six special libraries in the twin cities of Hyderabad and Secunderabad.
(Guide : B.P. Shenoy). 1718

Tasneem (Anwar Sultana).
Library research : A critical examination of

Entry No.

paradigmatic bases.
(Guide : M.V. Venugopal). 1719

Veena (K.).
International Information Systems for Agricultural Sciences and Technology (AGRIS).
(Guide : R.K. Gupta). 1720

PUNJAB UNIVERSITY, MLIS DISSERTATIONS 1984-85

	Entry No.
Dalip Singh. Reference toois in Punjabi : A technical study.	1721
Grover (Kiran Nisha). Science periodicals in India : A quantitative appraisal.	1722
Jagdip Kaur. Library cooperation in Great Britain and its lessons for India.	1723
Kainth (Jit Singh). Ranganathan's methodology of devising depth schedules : A case study with a specific subject.	1724
Kapoor (Sunita). Criteria and methedology for evaluating the effectiveness of reference and information functions in academic libraries with special reference to Northern India.	1725
Khurana (Parveen). Financing of college libraries in Chandigarh : A survey.	1726
Kulbir Kaur. Subject headings in 'Library Literature' : An analytical study.	1727
Malik (Virender). From Williamson to Conant : A critical study of education of librarians.	1728
Negi (Narbada Devi). Contribution of D.J. Foskett in the field of library classification.	1729
Pyarelal. Social sciences periodicals in Chandigarh research libraries : A users study.	1730

Entry No.

Singh (Ram Rattan).
Education Reform Commissions : Impact of their recommendations on the development of university libraries in India from 1857 A.D. onwards. 1731

Sabharwal (Seema).
Organiszation and utilization of Haryana Vidhan Sabha Library, Chandigarh : A cost-benefit study. 1732

Satinder Kaur.
International Standard Serial Number (ISSN) : Its current use by the publishers and related problems for the third world. 1733

Sharma (M.P.).
Bibliographic control and services in India : A survey and study with special reference to the role of the National Library. 1734

Tandon (Neelima).
Doctoral and Master's Degree dissertations in Anthropology submitted to the Punjab University, Chandigarh (1960-1984) : A bibliometric study. 1735

Thakar (G.S.).
A survey of users' attitudes towards the resources and services of three university libraries in Northern India. 1736

Trishanjit Kaur.
Social sciences periodicals in India : A quantitative appraisal. 1737

Uday Kumar.
Coordinate indexing : An experiment with "A" literature. 1738

UNIVERSITY OF POONA, MLIS DISSERTATIONS
1982-83

Entry No.

Kapadia (N.S.).
An academic library system for Poona : A study.
(Guide : M.R. Riswadkar). 1739

Majumdar (K.J.).
Education for librarianship in Gujarat : Retrospect, present and prospect.
(Guides : D.W. Shewde and M.R. Riswadkar). 1740

Shreshtha (K.B.).
Comprehensive library service for Nepal.
(Guide : M.R. Riswadkar). 1741

1983-84

Dalvi (V.S.).
Information seeking habits of the scientists at the National Chemical Laboratory, Pune.
(Guide : M.R. Riswadkar). 1742

Kamble (B.N.).
Problems in rendering library services by government aided public libraries in Pune district.
(Guide : D.W. Shewde). 1743

Shukla (M.C.).
Coverage of the immunology literature in *Biological Abstracts/Chemical Abstracts* and *Excerpta Medica* : A study in overlap, time lag and Indian contribution.
(Guide : M.R. Riswadkar). 1744

Singh (L.G.).
Development of libraries in Manipur State.
(Guide : S.G. Mahajan). 1745

Tamberwade (V.G.).
Resources and services of agricultural libraries in

Entry No.

Maharashtra : A survey.
(Guide : M.R. Riswadkar). 1746

1984-85

Joshi (Mona).
Microforms as an alternative to space requirement for periodicals backfiles in Jayakar Library.
(Guide : M.R. Riswadkar). 1747

Karande (A.G.).
Use of print media in technology transfer in Animal Husbandry.
(Guide : M.R. Riswadkar). 1748

Konkar (Seema).
Dissemination services of special libraries in Pune.
(Guide : M.R. Riswadkar). 1749

Natekar (Milan G.).
Use of periodicals in Jayakar library.
(Guide : S.G. Mahajan). 1750

VIKRAM UNIVERSITY, MLIS DISSERTATIONS 1984-85

Entry No.

Arjun Lal.
Rajendra Agricultural University Library, Pusa (Bihar) : Users' survey.
(Guide : G.D. Bhargava). 1751

Bairathi (Sharada).
Faculty attitude towards library services in Delhi University Library System.
(Guide : S.S. Agrawal). 1752

Bhatkhande (Surekha).
Cumulative index of Annals of Library Science and Documentation, (1958-1982).
(Guide : S.S. Agrawal). 1753

Charan (S.M.).
Library movement in Gujarat State : A review.
(Guide : G.D. Bhargava). 1754

Galnimkar (Sandhya).
Union catalogue of applied sciences, humanities and social science periodicals.
(Guide : S.S. Agrawal). 1755

Khatri (Tulsidas).
Cumulative index of ILA Bulletin, 1965-1983.
(Guide : S.S. Agrawal). 1756

Sarkar (Barun).
Bhagalpur university library, Bhagalpur : Users' survey.
(Guide : G.D. Bhargava). 1757

Sharma (Anita).
Technical services of special libraries of Bhopal city : Users' survey.
(Guide : G.D. Bhargava). 1758